Unexplained Michigan Mysteries

Gary Barfknecht

Friede Publications

*Friede Publications
P.O. Box 217
Davison, MI 48423-0217*

Printed in the United States of America

*First Printing, September 1993
Second Printing, November 1993
Third Printing, October 1995
Fourth Printing, October 2000
Fifth Printing, December 2002*

Cover design by Gail Dennis

ISBN 0-923756-05-1

CONTENTS

AUTHOR'S NOTE

I am educated as a scientist and both by training and personality am used to analyzing observable evidence and measurable data. And while connecting the dots between those specks of reality doesn't always form a clear picture, it does set up boundaries within which we can rationally postulate or speculate.

Much of what's in *Unexplained Michigan Mysteries* — unsolved murders, missing persons, and Great Lakes mysteries, for instance — lies comfortably within those borders.

Some topics, however — UFOs, ghosts, Bigfoot and paranormal phenomena, for examples — leave earthly parameters behind as they launch into the realm of the incredible and the untenable. Many people easily and quickly embrace one or more of those "alternate realities." My rational, skeptical makeup, however, clashes with the unbelievability or unprovability of those kinds of concepts.

But that doesn't matter, because *Unexplained Michigan Mysteries* is not about believability or even truth. Truth — difficult enough to discern in the everyday happenings of our "normal" lives — is by definition impossible to determine in any mystery, whether factual or fantastic.

Unexplained Michigan Mysteries presents — without either endorsing or debunking — a sampling of the kinds of fascinating, strange, incredible, sometimes-eerie experiences suffered or enjoyed by people in your state, your city, your neighborhood, perhaps next door.

INTRODUCTION

Unexplained Michigan Mysteries is a collection of 70 stories about some very strange happenings in Michigan. They span from prehistory to the present, and they range from the understandable to the unbelievable.

That covers a lot of territory, so obviously this book is by no means all-inclusive or in-depth. Rather, it's an eclectic cross section. Each of the 11 chapters exposes a different plane of the multi-faceted Michigan unknown. The stories used to scratch the surface of each of those fascinating areas of mystery were selected because they are representative, famous, sensational or otherwise significant.

All are uniquely informative and entertaining.

STRANGE ACCIDENTS AND INCIDENTS

Surprising incidents, occasionally accidents, often interrupt our carefully planned lives. Sometimes they're funny, most often they're annoying, and in a few instances they're tragic. But no matter what unexpected situations we encounter, we're usually able to deal with them because they are understandable or at least explainable.

Some Michigan residents, however, have been caught up in startling circumstances that turn out to be unexplainable, even incomprehensible.

WHAT BURNED BILLY?

At 7:40 p.m. on Sunday, December 13, 1959, a passing motorist noticed smoke wisping from Billy T. Preston's garage and notified the Pontiac Fire Department. Five minutes later firefighters arrived to discover Preston's dead body, sitting upright behind the steering wheel of his closed car, its engine still running. A flexible pipe had been attached to the car's exhaust system and run through the partially open front passenger side window. Directly below where the pipe released its deadly fumes, a small patch of the car seat smoldered. It looked like an "ordinary" suicide, that is until the firefighters got a closer look at Preston's body. They were surprised and puzzled to see that his face and arms were badly burned.

The victim was taken to Pontiac General Hospital, where doctors who performed an autopsy made even more-startling discoveries. They determined that Preston had, in fact, died of carbon monoxide poisoning. But for no reason connected to the way he died, Preston's back, legs and arms were covered with third-degree burns; his genitals were charred to a crisp; and his ears, nose, throat and lungs were seared. Yet the fully dressed victim's clothing — even his underwear — was not scorched or in any other way damaged. And more shocking, the body hair, including eyebrows and top of the head, was also unharmed. Unsinged hairs protruded out of charred flesh. The doctors said it was the strangest burn case they'd ever seen.

Police suspected a torture killing followed by a cover-up attempt to make the death look like a suicide. Someone might have undressed Billy, they speculated, then tortured him by fire, redressed him and placed him, still alive, in his car to die minutes later, an apparent suicide.

But that theory quickly fell apart. If someone had staged the suicide, he certainly had taken some elaborate steps. Investigators found that the car's tail pipe had been shortened to permit hooking on the flexible pipe that entered the car. Doctors added that Billy was so severely and extensively burned — skin literally fell off his left arm — that no one could have dressed him. And most importantly, there hadn't been enough time to carry out such an involved torture/ suicide plan. Preston had left his mother at his uncle's home at about 7 p.m., only 45 minutes before firefighters discovered his body.

Preston's mother said that her 27-year-old son, a welder at a GM plant, had been depressed over the state of his health for several months. He suffered from a serious kidney ailment and had been on sick leave for two months. The woman also said she had heard her son "puttering around" in his uncle's garage the evening of his death. Police checked and found the cut-off piece of tail pipe and another section of the flexible pipe in the garage of Billy's uncle. There was little doubt that Billy Preston had committed suicide.

What then had burned his flesh, yet left his hair and clothing entirely untouched?

Investigators said it must have been the heat from the exhaust or perhaps the burning upholstery that caused the unusual burns. But Preston's body was seated more than two feet away from the spot where the car seat had only smoldered, not burst into flames. And in the unlikely event that, from either the exhaust or the upholstery fire, the temperature in the car had risen high enough to cause third-degree burns, it certainly would also have burned Preston's hair and scorched his clothing.

There was only one explanation for the condition of Billy Preston's body. Somehow it had burned — cooked, if you will — from the inside out. But how was that possible? The only known method, the only known form of energy that could burn a body from the inside out without damaging hair or clothing is nuclear. But where and how could Billy Preston have been exposed to a megadose of nuclear radiation either in the one mile drive from his uncle's house or in his own garage?

He couldn't unless somehow his own body — perhaps as a final, violent reaction to its destruction — released a massive dose of nuclear radiation. Billy Preston might have been consumed by some sort of internal atomic explosion.

The idea sounds fantastic or absolutely absurd to most people, but not to investigators of the paranormal. They added Billy Preston's name to the list of more than 200 cases of "spontaneous human combustion" (SHC) that have been reported since the 17th century. In each case, say proponents of SHC, a human body burned — some to piles of ashes — without any known contact with an external source of fire and without damaging any surrounding objects such as furniture or clothing.

Scientists, however, flatly reject the theory of spontaneous human combustion and file away cases such as Billy Preston's under "puzzling," "unknown" or "unsolved." As a doctor who was on duty at Pontiac General the night Billy Preston's body was brought in said, "No explanation was available then, and so far as I know, none is now. I haven't seen a case like it since, and it is still baffling to me."

STRANGE LIGHTS OVER WATERSMEET

On a clear summer night in 1966, four bored Watersmeet teenagers decided to explore an uninhabited, seldom-visited area north of their small town. They turned their car onto a narrow dirt road that had first been cleared through the brush and trees during the Civil War. Like so many of the two-tracks that scratch the Upper Peninsula wilderness, this one was traveled only once or twice a year, usually by power company workers maintaining lines.

As the driver approached a section called Dog Meadow, he stopped the car to see if it was safe to continue through the swampy area. Suddenly, the inside of the car lit up as though a bright spotlight had been switched on. The four teens looked up through the windshield at a brilliant globe that appeared to rise slowly over the power line that paralleled the road. Frightened, the youths hurried back to town and reported the strange sight to the sheriff. By the time the sheriff arrived at Dog Meadow, the light had disappeared.

But not for long. The following night lights reappeared and have continued to do so almost every clear night since. Over the years thousands of area residents and tourists have viewed the eerie — some even say frightening — phenomenon.

At dusk cars park on the side of Robbins Pond Road, west of US-45, and people scramble to the summit of a nearby hill to watch the show. Not long after dark, what looks like a glowing ember appears to rise slowly out of the forest on the northwest horizon. As it moves low in the sky slowly to the northeast, the light increases in size and brilliance. Most observers say it looks like a bright star or a weather balloon. Sometimes the light splits and then comes back together after a few seconds. Finally, the glow shrinks to a spark, which then fades into the blackness. At two- to 15-minute intervals throughout the night, the light returns for a repeat performance.

Speculation about the lights' cause ranges from the supernatural to quasi-scientific.

Some area people claim the unusual shining is the spirit of a mail carrier who, along with his team of sled dogs, was ambushed and killed at Dog Meadow during the 1870s. Others say it's the ghost of a railroad engineer who, depending on who's telling the story, was either killed in an accident or murdered along the old railroad grade where the lights appear. Many who view the intense glow feel it has mystical or religious significance, and a few people have claimed that their car engines suddenly stopped running as the light passed over.

In the late 1970s, two New Jersey seismologists speculated that a minor earthquake in the area may have opened a small crack in the earth's crust. Radon, a radioactive gas associated with such faults, could be leaking out and glowing, they said. A scientist from Michigan Technological University, however, said that radon never appears luminous.

At about the same time, a team of investigators from the State Police, local sheriff's department, and utility company concluded that what was being observed were the headlights of automobiles traveling US-45 atop a distant hill. Between that hill and the hill from which the lights are viewed is an expansive swamp. At night the swamp releases latent heat in rising waves that distort the appearance and perspective of the headlights, said the investigators. Many area residents dismissed that explanation, too, saying that the unusual light appears year-round, including winter, when the swamp is frozen and covered with snow.

Though the cause of the light may be uncertain, its effect isn't. It will continue to draw crowds to the out-of-the-way patch of Upper Peninsula wilderness.

WANDA'S RAMBLING RAMBLER

Wanda Stanley purchased her American Motors Co. Rambler knowing that, while it wasn't flashy enough to attract much attention, it was reliable enough to just about guarantee no surprises. In January 1962, according to the book *Strange World*, Wanda's Rambler betrayed her on both counts.

Wanda returned home from an errand and parked her car, as she had done hundreds of times before, on the dead-level driveway next to her Dearborn house. As was her habit, she backed the car in, pulled the shift lever into low gear, then turned off the ignition, removed the key, got out, locked the doors, and went inside her house.

About ten minutes later, Wanda's excited neighbor called. He had been working in his front yard, he said, when he saw her Rambler — engine running — lurch forward and ease down the driveway. When it reached the street, the car turned left, accelerated down Dartmouth Avenue, sideswiped a traffic sign, and then, about a block away, turned sharply into a driveway where it rammed into another vehicle.

Wanda ran to the scene to find her Rambler, wheels still spinning, pushing against the other car like an aggressive football lineman. Wanda ran home, got her keys, ran back, unlocked her car, put the key into the ignition, and turned the car off — again.

Mechanics couldn't find any reason for the spontaneous joy ride, and it never happened again.

JUST DROPPED IN FOR LUNCH

On March 31, 1897, Galesburg residents were startled by a blinding white light that suddenly appeared in the sky over their village. Strange crackling noises pierced the air for several seconds, and then the light and sound disappeared.

For the next week and a half, area farmers reported that livestock had mysteriously disappeared or had been slaughtered by something unknown. Then, on April 10, a group of fishermen spotted a strange animal moving along the shore of Pine Lake. Though it looked like no creature they had ever seen, said the men, it did somewhat resemble a panther and made a terrible shrieking noise before disappearing into the woods.

The alien animal was not seen again, and there were no further unusual deaths or disappearances of farm animals.

THE RESTLESS BED

Many hotels and motels feature rooms furnished with vibrating beds. Plunk in a quarter or two, lie down, and gently shake for a few relaxing moments.

But what would you do if the bed in your home — which isn't supposed to — suddenly began shaking? According to a report in the *Pontiac Press*, that's exactly the extraordinary situation Cecile Kleino faced on February 1, 1960.

Early that Monday afternoon, Cecile, who was home alone, laid some freshly pressed laundry on her daughter's bed. As she started to turn away, the layers of sweaters and skirts began to gently sway. She moved closer to steady the pile, then jumped back startled. The laundry was moving because the bed was shaking.

When she couldn't find any reason why the bed should be vibrating, Cecile left the room, closed the door, and hoped it would stop. But when her 17-year-old daughter, Christine, arrived home from school a couple of hours later, the bed was still moving.

Husband Albert and 21-year-old son Dean got home from work soon after, listened to Cecile's incredulous story, then went to check for themselves. None of the other furniture in the room was moving, only the bed. Albert and Dean tried to get it to stop by holding it and sitting and lying on it. But the bed kept vibrating, so the family called the Pontiac police.

The young patrolman who answered the call took a quick look then hustled back to the station for advice. "I can't believe it," he told fellow officers. "I think I must be cracking up." The police decided to call in their fire fighting comrades for help.

When firefighters arrived at the Kleino home, the bed was still vibrating. The men lifted the bed, and as they moved it to another

7

part of the room, it quit shaking. But as soon as they set it down, it began vibrating again.

Finally, the police officer said, "Let's try taking it apart." At his words the bed instantly stopped vibrating. The firemen took it apart anyway and examined it carefully but couldn't find anything unusual. As soon as they finished putting the bed back together, it began shaking.

Then, as suddenly as it had started, the bed stopped. It never moved again.

WHAT CAUSED THE PLUNGE?

Gale-force winds pummeled Donald Klassen's semi as the Manitoba truck driver headed north across the Mackinac Bridge shortly after 6:30 p.m. on September 22, 1989. Rain had fallen off and on all day, and a spray hissed from his tires as he moved over the bridge's wet, outer paved lane. About 50 feet ahead of him, a blue Yugo hummed over the metal grating of the inner lane.

Suddenly the tiny Yugo slammed into the bridge's outer steel-post guardrail, vaulted atop the barrier, then dropped over the side. Klassen jammed on the truck's brakes, ran to the rail, and looked down to the cold, gray water 170 feet below. All he could see was a tire, an oil slick and some bubbles. Beneath the surface, the mangled mass of metal that was once the Yugo slowly, awkwardly tumbled toward the bottom. Its sole occupant, 31-year-old Leslie Pluhar, was critically injured and unconscious . . . but still breathing. As the wreckage came to rest on a rocky ledge 150 feet below the waves, Pluhar drowned.

Klassen and other witnesses who had joined him at the rail could do nothing but stare into the aftermath of one of the most statistically and tragically incredible accidents in Michigan highway history. The Mackinac Bridge had been open for 32 years. Sixty-five million vehicles had made the trip across. And yes, there had been accidents, most of them fender-benders and even three crashes that had resulted in fatalities. But never before that gloomy night had a car carried someone to his or her death over the edge of Michigan's best-known landmark.

How and why did the unthinkable happen? And, could it happen again?

The Michigan State Police, insurance companies, attorneys, the Mackinac Bridge Authority and its engineering firm, and House and Senate committees of the Legislature all launched their own intensive investigations to try to find the answers.

Based on the physical evidence and the testimony of several witnesses, there was little disagreement over *what* had happened. At about 6:40 p.m. Pluhar, a waitress from Royal Oak, steered her 1987 Yugo along I-75 onto the 5-mile-long bridge. She was headed north to Gould City, in the U.P., to see her new boyfriend and meet his mother for the first time. Lying on the back seat was a surprise gift, a stained-glass lamp she had bought for her friend's new apartment.

The bridge deck was wet from afternoon rain squalls, and strong northwest winds were gusting to 48 mph. Pluhar eased to the bridge's inside lane, made of open steel grating designed to let wind pass through and thus stabilize the mammoth structure.

As Pluhar's car passed the bridge's south tower, the vehicle suddenly swerved left and ran up onto and straddled the 2-foot-wide center median. The Yugo rattled over that 4-inch-high concrete strip for 70 feet, then rotated clockwise and skidded back across both northbound lanes. When the vehicle reached the edge of the bridge, the right front tire struck the 11-inch-high tubular-steel lower guardrail, then vaulted up onto the 38-inch-high iron-pipe outer barrier. The Yugo skidded atop the pipe for 45 feet, slammed into a suspension cable, dropped, and slid down a diagonal steel support girder to the bottom of the bridge superstructure.

Then, just seven seconds after the horror had begun, the nearly crushed car and its unconscious driver dropped silently to the water and disappeared into the depths.

But after collecting reams of data and volumes of testimony, the investigating groups and individuals could not come close to agreeing on *why* Pluhar's trip across the bridge had ended in spectacular tragedy.

Initially, the cause seemed obvious. A gale-force gust of wind had blown Pluhar's Yugo across the center median causing her to lose control. And another powerful blast may even have helped carry the ultralight vehicle up and over the side of the bridge. Said one witness, the car looked just "like a piece of paper being swept away in the wind."

But scientists testified that it was physically and aerodynamically impossible for the near-50-mph gusts to move the 1,800-pound Yugo even from side to side, let alone up and over the 3-foot-high railing.

Wind, however, may have been the reason Pluhar lost control of her car, said State Police investigators. When her subcompact was buffeted by a strong gust, Pluhar may have over-corrected in an attempt to regain control. Or, said investigators, she may have veered over the median while doing something as simple as bending over to pick up an object that had dropped onto the floor.

Pluhar also may have been driving too fast, especially for the wet conditions. After measuring skid marks on the pavement and impact marks on the railing, accident reconstruction experts calculated that the Yugo was moving at 55-63 mph. The speed limit on the bridge is 45 mph. A check of Pluhar's driving record revealed four speeding convictions, one drunken driving conviction, and two license suspensions plus one restriction between 1982 and 1984.

But Pluhar had had no tickets since her license was reinstated in February 1985. And several witnesses, including truck driver Klassen, estimated she was only going about 40-50 mph.

Whatever the reason Pluhar ended up straddling the median, once she got there she may have panicked. According to the final State Police report on the accident, she jammed her foot hard on the accelerator not the brake, which sent her car sliding out of control toward the edge of the bridge. Investigators found the imprint of the accelerator pedal pressed hard into the bottom of her right tennis shoe, and Klassen added that, "Even when she crossed the median, her brake lights did not come on."

Witnesses who were driving in the opposite direction, however, said they saw the front of the Yugo "nose down" as though the driver had put on the brakes. And it was possible, said some accident-reconstruction experts, that the accelerator imprint could have happened when she and the car slammed into the water.

Pluhar's family suspected that the car itself may have played a role in the accident. The ultra-light Yugoslavian-made Yugo had gained an international reputation as one of the worst cars ever made, in part because of problems with its steering and brakes.

Whatever nightmarish set of circumstances sent Leslie Pluhar's Yugo skidding out of control toward the edge of the bridge, why didn't the barrier keep her vehicle from going over?

Is the Mackinac Bridge inherently unsafe? Is every driver who crosses the span potentially risking the same fate as Leslie Pluhar?

A report by a Michigan Senate committee that investigated the accident answered "yes" to both. The bridge met safety standards of the 1950s, said the legislators, but not today's, especially the design of the outer guardrail. The committee cited a half dozen studies by some of the nation's most prestigious highway-design institutes. All condemned the use of low inner curb / high outer rail barriers like on the Mackinac Bridge. And all said that the inner low curb can act as a catapult when struck by a vehicle and help lift it over the outer rail.

What's needed to prevent a similar future tragedy, concluded the Senate committee, is to install modern, inward-curving barriers that would deflect errant vehicles back onto the roadway.

But such a change would not come cheaply and might, in fact, be structurally impossible. Without exhaustive engineering studies, nobody could say what destabilizing effects a new multimillion-dollar barrier might have on a structure that was intricately designed to withstand winds to "infinity."

Besides, said the Michigan House committee report, it's not necessary. It wasn't a "structural failure or flaw" in the bridge itself that caused Leslie Pluhar's death. At least five other vehicles, since the bridge's opening, had rammed into the guardrails but did not go through or over. What killed Pluhar, they concluded, was excessive speed. "As long as drivers stick to the 45 mph speed limit," stated the committee's report, "the Mackinac Bridge is the safest stretch of highway in Michigan."

Who's right? Who's wrong? What really caused one of the most spectacular auto accidents in state history?

Leslie Pluhar took most of the answers with her into the Straits of Mackinac.

MICHI-JAWS

Southern California swimmers watch for sharks that occasionally prowl the beach shallows. And Caribbean island tourists are sometimes on the receiving end of painful, often debilitating stings from Portugese men-of-war. Thank goodness we in Michigan don't have to worry about any dangerous denizens of our deeps. Or do we?

William Hart probably didn't think so, at least until he went on a 1982 holiday fishing trip to Gull Lake, near Richland. The 23-year-old Kalamazoo man and his friends hadn't tossed lines for long on Saturday, July 3rd, when Hart pulled out a strange-looking green-and-black, red-bellied fish. As he removed the hook from his catch, the foot-long fish attacked the pliers in his hand.

Neither Hart nor his buddies had any idea what he had caught, and it took nearly two weeks to find out. Hart first took the fish to several pet shops. When none of the store owners could identify the fish, he brought it to the nearest Department of Natural Resources office, and they finally informed him that he had caught . . . a piranha.

Yes, a live piranha. You know, the tiny one-pound Amazon butcher shop, a school of which can reduce a large animal to bones in minutes and, at least in movies, do the same to humans.

Hart's catch had to be a freak, one-in-a-million twist of fate, said a DNR spokesman. Someone must have dumped the piranha into the lake from an aquarium shortly before Hart hooked it because, assured the expert, the tropical fish certainly couldn't live more than a couple of hours in the cold water. Fish dealers around the state agreed, adding that the brightly colored fish would also fall easy victim to pike, muskies and other predators.

So that was the end of the excitement, until August 1987 when — same area, different lake — Betty Moreland caught Piranha II. Moreland said that, when the fish bared its needle-like teeth, she *knew* what she had pulled from Pine Creek Lake, west of Otsego. DNR officials confirmed her identification and speculated that, again, someone had illegally emptied an aquarium. But this time the DNR spokesman said that piranha couldn't survive — not just a couple of hours — but over the *winter* in Michigan waters.

The DNR changed its story again when, in April 1989, George Kearney pulled Piranha III from the Huron River near Ford Motor

Company's Ypsilanti assembly plant. This time Dr. Ned Fogle, of the DNR fisheries division, was quoted as saying, "Most tropical fish can't survive Michigan's winters unless they remain near areas where heated water is discharged. But we really don't know. If they found a mate and started reproducing, we don't know what could happen."

How many piranhas have been illegally introduced into Michigan lakes, ponds and rivers? How many have survived to breed? No one can say for sure, but probably not many, if any. And besides, all a piranha would do to a person is inflict a painful nip, not strip flesh to the bone. So say the experts . . . the same kind of experts who said piranhas couldn't survive in Michigan.

UNUSUAL POWERS

Natural physical laws set quantifiable limits to what most of us can perceive and do.

A few Michiganians, however, apparently have not been confined within the boundaries that define our "normal" world. They seem to have abilities beyond the rest of us. They appear to receive stimuli differently than most of us, or perhaps they perceive different stimuli. What they have apparently done is not understandable and therefore — because we reject what we don't understand — is usually judged unbelievable.

OUT OF SIGHT, INTO MIND

Kalkaska County Sheriff Alan Hart didn't flat out reject the idea of psychic power or doubt the sincerity of people who claimed to have it. It was just that, in his experience, any information he'd ever received from such unorthodox sources had been too vague and general to be of much use. So in late November 1977, when three psychics showed up from various parts of Lower Michigan and offered their help in locating a missing deer hunter, Hart was politely indifferent.

The two men and one woman, who had met each other for the first time only days before at a "psychic fair," handed the sheriff a piece of paper containing two drawings. Only one person had done the rough sketches, they said, but the other two had agreed that's what they also saw. The three also insisted that no matter what resulted from their images they wanted to remain anonymous. Sheriff Hart agreed and thanked them. After they left, the sheriff glanced at the paper, then handed it to his deputy, Steven Linn, without comment. Hart then rejoined the intensive search for 15-year-old Larry Wyckoff.

During a snowstorm the day after Thanksgiving, Wyckoff had spotted a wounded four-point buck crossing the road in southcentral Kalkaska County where he was hunting. Wyckoff walked the short distance back to his hunting party's camp, got a buddy, and together they followed the deer into the woods. The driving snow made tracking difficult, however, and Wyckoff's friend decided to head out of the woods. He urged Wykoff to join him. But the Warren youth, anxious to tag his first deer ever, said he wanted to continue stalking the animal. "Don't worry," he said. "I won't get lost."

When Wyckoff didn't return to the camp by dark, the other members of his hunting party walked up and down the road where he had entered the woods, firing their guns into the air and shouting. But the heavy snowfall and thick forest seemed to swallow all sounds. The group didn't hear Wyckoff shoot or shout in return, so they contacted the sheriff's office. The temperature that night dropped to 5 degrees Farenheit.

The next morning Sheriff Hart and several deputies combed the area where Wyckoff had gone after the deer. When they, too, turned up no sight or sound of the young hunter, Sheriff Hart put out a call for volunteers for a search party.

Nearly 200 people, most of them local residents, responded. Over the next several weeks, they spent thousands of man-hours walking a variety of patterns over eight to 10 square miles of near-wilderness surrounding the spot where Wyckoff was last seen. At the same time, government and private airplanes repeatedly criss-crossed the area.

During the ground search, Deputy Linn showed the psychics' sketches to several locals he knew who were familiar with that section of the county. One drawing depicted an unusually shaped tree, and the other showed a body lying on its back in a ravine. No one Linn showed the sketches to recognized the landmarks, however, so he put the paper in a desk drawer at his office and forgot about it.

Heavy snows soon buried the area, stalling the massive search, which had turned up no sign of Larry Wyckoff. Over the winter two Traverse City men organized a second, even larger search that was to involve the Michigan National Guard, the Coast Guard, and up to 1,000 volunteers. Although there was speculation that Wyckoff may have used the incident to run away from his family, most authorities expected to discover and recover a body. The search was scheduled for mid-May, when the woods would be mostly clear of snow.

In early May, Steve Linn was cleaning out his office desk when he came across the sketches the psychics had drawn. For reasons he could never explain, Linn suddenly realized he had neglected to show the drawings to Charlie Stuck, a 71-year-old lifelong hunter and trapper who had a reputation of being *the* best woodsmen in the area.

At 4 p.m. on Sunday May 7, Linn pulled his patrol car up to Stuck's house in the near-ghost town of Sharon. Linn laid the paper containing the psychics' sketches on the vehicle's hood and asked Stuck if he'd ever seen such a place.

Rubbing the stubble on his chin, Stuck studied the paper for only seconds and then looked up at Linn. The lines in his weathered face formed a shock pattern. "I know right where it is," he exclaimed. "I can walk right to it." The sketches, Stuck explained, showed a knoll and a filled-in pond that beavers had created more than 100 years before. It wasn't far from his home, he said, and was in the general

17

area where Wyckoff had been hunting. "Let's go find him," Stuck said. "I have a feeling."

Stuck directed Linn to drive southwest from Sharon down John Road. A few miles later, they stopped and headed east into the woods directly to the place Stuck thought was depicted on the psychics' sketches. It was a low, rolling wooded area only about three-quarters of a mile off the road but more than two miles from the point where Wyckoff had begun his pursuit of the deer. When darkness ended their search a couple of hours later, they had failed to find Wyckoff's body.

Stuck was certain they were in the right spot, though, and so at about 11:30 the next morning he and Linn returned, this time in the company of Allen Cross, a 43-year-old animal control officer who was also familiar with the swampy area. A half hour later, Stuck shouted to the other two. He had found Wyckoff's partially decomposed body facing upwards under a leafless birch tree on the slope of a shallow ravine. An autopsy later determined that the youth had frozen to death. When Stuck and Linn had searched the day before, they had missed seeing the body by only 10 yards. The closest anyone in the search party the previous fall had come, it turned out, was a quarter-mile. And though the body was somewhat exposed in a relatively thinly wooded area, the blue plaid jacket, blue jeans, and dark blue snowmobile boots worn by Wyckoff had camouflaged his body from aerial view.

Several hours later, as Wyckoff's body was carried from the woods, Linn pulled the psychics' paper from his jacket pocket and looked around him. The position of Wyckoff's body when found and the surrounding topography were strikingly similar to what was depicted in the bottom sketch. And the lone, oddly shaped tree detailed in the top drawing? About 30 feet north of the site of the body stood just such a uniquely formed tree.

"I'm skeptical about these things," Linn was later quoted as saying, "but when someone can pick out that spot in a 10,000-acre area by looking at the sketches, there just has to be something to it."

FEELING BLUE

When Ann (Morrow) Compton of Flint first discovered her unusual ability, she was too self-conscious and embarrassed to realize what a rare, remarkable power she possessed. As a senior at Owensboro (Kentucky) High School in 1939, Ann Morrow was called upon to help her math teacher in a classroom demonstration of the laws of probability. The teacher blindfolded Morrow, handed her two card-size pieces of construction paper — one red and one blue — and asked her to guess which was which. Morrow identified the colors correctly, and the teacher explained to the class that it wasn't surprising since there was a 1 in 2, or 50:50 chance of being right.

The teacher then added a green card, shuffled the cards, and again asked Morrow to guess the colors. Again Morrow did. The teacher added a black card and shuffled. Again Morrow defied the laws of chance by correctly identifying the colors of all four cards. Surprised at Morrow's incredible run of "luck," her teacher called in the school's psychology teacher, Marion Gillim, to watch. The math teacher added a fifth card, this time another blue card.

Just as Morrow again identified all five cards correctly, the lunch bell rang, much to everyone's relief. The frustrated teacher was glad her failed demonstration had ended, and shy, modest Ann Morrow was grateful she was no longer the focus of attention. Foremost in her mind after the unusual incident was to brush and restyle her hair, which had been tousled from the blindfold.

The incident was soon forgotten by all involved, and Ann Morrow went on to live a normal life. She married Alan Compton in 1945, and soon after, when Alan obtained work at a General Motors factory, the couple moved to the Detroit area. Ten years later they moved to Flint when Alan became an inspector at the Ternstedt Plant in that city. Mrs. Compton worked a few hours each weekday as a school bus driver and spent most of the rest of her time tending to her four sons and the family's large garden. One night a week she bowled in a league.

Then in early 1963 Mrs. Compton's comfortable routine was interrupted by a surprising phone call from Dr. Richard P. Youtz, a psychology professor at Barnard College, New York. Youtz had carefully followed reports coming out of Russia about a woman there

19

who allegedly could identify colors with her fingertips. When Youtz mentioned his interest to a colleague, Dr. Marion Gillim, she recalled how she may have watched a girl at Owensboro High School do the same thing nearly 25 years before. Dr. Gillim then traced Ann Morrow Compton's whereabouts through Ann's mother, who still lived in Owensboro, and gave the phone number to Dr. Youtz.

Youtz asked Mrs. Compton if he could travel to Flint and test her potentially remarkable capabilities. Mrs. Compton had all but forgotten how she had once convincingly violated the laws of probability, and she had never mentioned the experience to her husband or children. After this long a time, she told Dr. Youtz, she had no idea if she would still be able to "see" colors with her fingers. And if she did, the last thing the quiet, reserved woman wanted was the kind of international attention that surrounded the Russian woman. Mrs. Compton did not want to become a sideshow freak in a media circus.

Youtz explained that his interest was strictly in research that might someday help sightless people. Perhaps, he speculated, Mrs. Compton possessed an ability that could be determined and analyzed and then taught to or developed by others as a substitute for vision with the eyes. And when Dr. Youtz assured Mrs. Compton that he would conduct his tests in secrecy and that he would only publish the results in scholarly journals, she consented.

From April to August 1963, Youtz paid several visits to the Compton home, staying anywhere from two days to three weeks each time. Using equipment he had specially built, he performed a battery of tests on Mrs. Compton's tactile color-sensing abilities.

Youtz began by performing a more-sophisticated version of the high school math teacher's demonstration. Compton was blindfolded with a sleeping mask and seated before a black 2- by 3-foot plywood box. Leading out of the front panel of the box were two black velveteen armholes into which her hands were fitted. Through a door in the back of the box Dr. Youtz placed three cards, one with a red square on it and the other two with blue squares. To ensure a consistent texture, Dr. Youtz covered the cards with a thin piece of transparent plastic. He then closed the door and sealed the box so that there was no light inside.

Youtz then asked Mrs. Compton to pick two cards of the same color and name the colors. Mrs. Compton ran her fingers over the plastic shield, indicated two of the cards, and said they were blue. Youtz repeated the procedure five times, mixing the cards up each time. Mrs. Compton never saw the cards, and Youtz didn't tell her if her answers were right or wrong. Compton named the cards correctly all five times.

Youtz repeated the experiment several times with a variety of colors — red, yellow, green, purple, white and black — and Mrs. Compton never missed. She was able to correctly sense colors even while wearing thin plastic, rubber or cotton gloves. She could not identify the color of objects submerged in warm water, however, nor could she discern colors when the temperature of her fingertips fell below 75 degrees Fahrenheit. Also, when presented with extreme subtleties — a pale yellow and white, for instance — Mrs. Compton was unable to differentiate the colors.

When he was done, Youtz was convinced that Mrs. Compton could literally feel colors with her fingertips. Trouble was, in spite of the barrage of tests, the professor still had no idea how. Mrs. Compton could not explain how she did what she did. She did say that light colors felt smooth and thin and that dark colors felt thick and heavy. But she could not explain how she was able to distinguish one dark color from another dark color or one light color from another light color.

As a result Youtz was unable to determine or explain the physiology, psychology or perhaps parapsychology behind Mrs. Compton's unique power. It simply couldn't be explained. Similar experiments with the Russian woman revealed that her color-sensing abilities were "dubious." Youtz abandoned any hope of applying Mrs. Compton's unusual tactile abilities to some useful purpose and moved on to other kinds of research.

Someone, however, leaked the details of Youtz's experiments, and much to her dismay, Mrs. Compton was the center of mainstream media attention for a short time.*

When the publicity subsided, Mrs. Compton resumed her role as a Flint housewife, not letting the fact the she evidently was one of a kind in the world change her life.

---

*Out of respect for Mrs. Compton's continuing desire for privacy, her real name was not used in this account.

DISTANT WARNING

Most of us, at one time or another, have been struck with the sudden, uneasy "gut-feeling" that something bad was about to happen to someone we love. It's especially frustrating, even agonizing, when the person in our thoughts is somewhere that makes it impossible to communicate with them. Helpless, we can only sit and wait until we hear that they're alright.

Ken Howell, too, had no choice but to sit. But he didn't wait.

Mary Howell had spent a pleasant week in the spring of 1962 visiting with her son, Ken, and his family at their Lansing home. But she was anxious to get back to her Grand Ledge area farmhouse, and late Sunday evening prepared to leave. "Please stay another night, Mom," implored Ken. "I don't know why, but I have a feeling it's dangerous for you to travel."

Mary tried to convince her son there was no reason for concern. The rain that had fallen all week had stopped, and Mary reminded Ken that the 20-mile route back to her farm was so familiar she could "drive it blindfolded."

In spite of Ken's continued protests, Mary headed for Grand Ledge. As she turned onto the little-traveled road that led the last mile to her home, she thought how relieved Ken would be when she called to tell him what a routine trip it had been. But only a few hundred yards farther, Mary headed her car into fog so thick it muted sounds and limited vision to only inches. But Mary kept slowly moving along the narrow gravel road, confident that her driveway would still be easy to locate. It was exactly a half mile from a bridge she would soon cross. Mary glanced down at her dashboard clock, curious as to how long the normally two-minute trip would take. The clock read 9:30 p.m.

When Mary looked back up through her windshield, she was surprised to see a red light glowing through the dark haze a few yards ahead of her. "How strange," she thought. It looked like a traffic signal, but it hadn't been there when she had traveled the road the week before. And there sure wasn't enough traffic on the road to justify installing one, she thought.

Still, she stopped and waited for the light to turn green. After several minutes, when the light still hadn't changed, Mary inched the car forward. The light suddenly disappeared, and she heard a voice shout, "Stop!"

Mary again stopped, turned off the engine, and got out to check. As she walked forward, she began to make out the sounds of rushing water. Then only 10 feet from her car's front bumper, she stood at the site of the bridge. Except the bridge was no longer there. A flash flood had turned the normally shallow creek into a raging torrent that had washed away the turn-of-the-century wood structure.

As Mary stood trembling, a sheriff's car pulled up. The officer made sure Mary was all right and then asked, "What made you stop, lady? In this pea-soup fog, there's no way you could have seen the bridge was out."

"I think my son warned me," she said, and then told the deputy about her strange experience, finishing with, "You probably think I'm a mental case, don't you?"

"No . . . no I don't, lady," he replied. "In fact, it's only because I kind of believe in that ESP stuff that I'm here. None of the other guys back at the department wanted to respond to the call we got earlier."

"What call was that?" asked Mary.

"Oh, they said some crackpot named Ken from Lansing called at 9:30 and insisted he'd just had a vision that his mother was in danger of drowning out here on this road."

20:20 MINDSIGHT

Mattie stood trembling at Anita Turner's door. The day before, Labor Day 1982, Mattie had watched a neighbor woman leave her west-Detroit apartment in the grip of a man. Though the young woman was not struggling, something about the scene had bothered Mattie. When her neighbor hadn't returned by the next afternoon, Mattie went to Anita Turner for help.

Mattie had never met Turner and only knew her by reputation. Turner, the divorced mother of four grown children, was well known in the area as a psychic. And for good reason.

For many years she had demonstrated an uncanny ability to make specific, accurate predictions, not the vague generalities of most self-proclaimed parlor "psychics." And she always did so without ever subtly fishing for clues. When an acquaintance once complained his car had just been stolen, Turner correctly told him exactly when and where he would recover it. She also predicted the hair color, complexion and partial address of the killer of a Detroit woman's out-of-town cousin. Turner even correctly told the woman she would ride back to Detroit from the funeral with the murderer, whom police later determined to be another family member. A Chicago woman who ran for the Illinois State Senate admitted she lost the election because she ignored Turner's very specific — but at the time, puzzling and seemingly unnecessary — campaign advice. And a prominent Detroit attorney has so much confidence in Turner's ability to "read people," she regularly uses Turner to assist with jury selection.

So Mattie, thinking such a prominent woman would likely have nothing to do with her apparently insignificant, vague worry, nervously pushed the doorbell. Turner answered and after listening intently to Mattie's concern, invited her in. Turner was very soft-spoken, low-key, almost shy — nothing at all, thought Mattie, like someone who possessed "special powers." In an apparent ice-breaking gesture, Turner even asked Mattie some questions about her family.

Turner, as it turned out, had had an almost immediate, chilling vision, and she was making sure Mattie wasn't related to the missing woman before revealing it. Turner then told Mattie that she saw a woman being led through a field, and that she heard three gunshots. A body would be found, said Turner, within 10 blocks of Mattie's flat near a gray building marked with the initials, M.I.D. Behind the building, she said, was a fenced field and railroad tracks. She also said she saw the figure "10" and the letters, G.W.E.N. Stunned, Mattie told Turner, for the first time, that the missing woman's first name was Gwendolyn.

Within a day Mattie called Turner to say she thought she had found the location. But she was too afraid to look for a body, yet too embarrassed to call the police. So, on September 9, three days after the apparent abduction, Turner herself made the call.

Detroit police officers from the 10th (Livernois) Precinct drove to the 1000 block of Doris St. and parked in front of the abandoned Mid-American Building. They searched the area close to the building but found no body, so they contacted Turner.

Turner told them to look in the field behind the building. Police then tromped through the large, overgrown lot that was bounded by railroad tracks and vacant warehouses. About 100 feet from the street, they spotted a body lying in tall weeds in a slight depression. The victim had been shot three times in the head and upper body. It was Mattie's neighbor, 23-year-old Gwendolyn Scott.

A subsequent investigation resulted in the arrest of the victim's husband, Allan Scott, who was tried and convicted of kidnapping and murder and sentenced to life in prison. The same investigation verified that Anita Turner had known nothing about the victim or the crime except through her visions. And the police officers involved, all of whom said they didn't believe in psychics, admitted that had it not been for Anita Turner's "special abilities," they might never have discovered the body.

THE PAW PAW FIRE BREATHER

In 1882 a new patient walked into Dr. L.C. Woodman's Paw Paw office with an ailment no physician had seen before and probably none has since. Twenty-seven-year-old A. W. Underwood told Dr. Woodman he was able to start fires with his breath and had been able to do so for 15 years. Sometimes it was an advantage, he admitted, like when he got cold while out hunting and had no matches. He would gather dry leaves and twigs and then breathe on them to start a fire.

But most of the time, complained Underwood, his unusual power caused problems. If he wasn't careful where he breathed, he started unwanted fires. Just the night before at supper, while wiping his mouth after swallowing a glass of water, he had set his napkin ablaze, he said.

Underwood then demonstrated. He took Dr. Woodman's cotton handkerchief and held it tightly against his mouth while breathing through it. In a few seconds the cloth burst into flames and then completely burned.

Though Underwood appeared unassuming and sincere, Dr. Woodman, not surprisingly, suspected a trick or a hoax. He asked Underwood if he would subject himself to thorough examination and testing. Underwood said yes, and so over the next several weeks, Dr. Woodman and several colleagues checked everything they could think of to see if "humbug" was involved. They poked and probed Underwood's mouth and teeth. They asked him to strip, rinse out his mouth with various solutions, wash his hands, and even put on surgeon's rubber gloves.

Underwood still was consistently able to set newspapers, envelopes and other paper aflame with only his breath. He could only do it twice a day, however, and would then sink into a chair exhausted. After one such session, Dr. Woodman placed his hand on Underwood's head and observed that the scalp was "violently twitching, as if under intense excitement."

Convinced that Underwood's bizarre power was real, Dr. Woodman sought an explanation and help via articles in the *Michigan Medical News* and *Scientific American* magazine. But no one offered a suggestion for either a cause or a cure.

For a brief time, Underwood took advantage of his unique power by performing for the residents of Paw Paw — setting fires on demand for a fee. But the novelty soon wore off, and the fire breather lived out the remainder of his life as normally as he could.

EXTRAORDINARY DREAMS

We all dream, and most of us realize that we dream. But more often than not, within minutes of waking, we forget the private, neuron-generated nighttime videos that just played in our brains.

That's because dreams usually aren't very memorable or, for that matter, very meaningful. A few researchers believe that dreams can reflect deep subconscious wishes or fears. Most experts, however, say that dreams are rarely more than a metaphorical, albeit sometimes bizarre or surrealistic, replay of the issues, events and people we deal with in our daily lives. Dreaming is a way for the mind to sort through and process the bombardment of stimuli it receives while awake.

On rare occasions, this routine, subconscious psychological housecleaning results in an extraordinary rearrangement of waking lives.

LOVE TURNED COLD

For more than three years following her mother Dorothy's 1985 disappearance, a recurring nightmare haunted Kelly Tyburski. Her dream was short, simple and terrifyingly consistent. She saw her mother tied up, locked, or otherwise confined in an amorphous place from which she couldn't escape. Kelly didn't know where it was, and her mother wasn't able to tell her. And what bothered Kelly almost as much as the dream itself was that there really wasn't any reason for it. When her mother vanished, it wasn't all that surprising to Kelly or the rest of her family.

For 17 years the Tyburskis — Dorothy, Leonard, and their two daughters, Kelly and Kim — led an apparently normal, middle-class suburban life in their ranch-style home in Canton Township. Forty-one-year-old Leonard spent all of his married years working at Detroit's Mackenzie High School, first as a science teacher then as an administrator. Thirty-seven-year-old Dorothy, according to neighbors, was a "typical housewife" and a pleasant though somewhat distant person who always seemed happy. For recreation Dorothy and Leonard bowled together in a local league. The entire family loved animals and worked together to take care of their exotic birds, rabbits, ducks, skunks, raccoons and other pets.

But in 1984 the Tyburski family began to fall apart. When her sister died in February, Dorothy complained of depression, then suffered a nervous breakdown, according to Leonard. Twelve-year-old Kim and 16-year-old Kelly became upset because their mother began "behaving like a teenager." Dorothy regularly flirted with Kelly's 17-year-old boyfriend, Craig Albright, and even made explicit sexual references about him. In mid-September 1985 Albright came to live with the Tyburskis after being thrown out of his grandmother's house.

A week after Albright had moved into the house, Leonard placed a 2 a.m. call to the Canton Township Fire Rescue Unit for help. His wife, he reported, had taken an overdose of pills in an apparent suicide attempt and had left the house on foot. Rescuers found Dorothy wandering in a field and took her to a nearby hospital emergency room. Her stomach was pumped, and she was released the following morning.

A week later Dorothy disappeared. Leonard told Kelly and Kim that he and their mother had had a terrible argument and that she had left, permanently, with nothing but "the clothes on her back." Leonard reported his wife missing to the Canton Township Police, and Craig Albright moved out of the house.

Police investigated and found nothing to indicate foul play. Neighbors said they weren't surprised to find out Dorothy had left. Most had heard rumors of marital problems, and a few said Dorothy had complained to them about her marriage. Neighborhood gossip even had it that Dorothy had called home and requested that some of her personal belongings be dropped off at a freeway rest area. In 1987 Leonard took and passed a lie detector test. This was obviously a case of someone who had left, didn't want to have contact, and didn't want to come back.

Leonard, Kelly and Kim tried to resume their lives as best they could. For several months the normally outgoing Leonard was tense, quiet and withdrawn, but then he gradually became more relaxed and friendlier than ever. Kelly graduated from high school and then enrolled at Michigan State University.

Kelly didn't talk much to her dorm roommates about her mother's disappearance. But she often woke them with her screams and cries as her nightmare — her mother lying helpless somewhere, with no hope of escape — became more frequent and more vivid.

On January 2, 1989, during a Christmas-break visit to her home, a sudden, sickening suspicion meshed with Kelly's darkest dreams. At about 1 p.m. Kelly slowly walked down the basement stairs and toward a locked 15-cubic-foot chest-type freezer she and her sister had passed countless times on their way to take care of their birds or play on a drum set. Using a screwdriver she probed, jimmied and pried the lock. Finally it snapped open, and she slowly raised the lid. Kelly saw splatters of blood caked on the freezer walls and then looked down upon her mother's frozen body, lying on its right side, legs drawn up in fetal position, on top of frozen meat wrapped in brown butcher paper.

Kelly somehow maintained her composure, ran upstairs, got Kim, and called a friend to drive them to the police station. As they left the house, Leonard arrived, but his daughters rushed past him without saying anything.

When police arrived, Leonard confessed that on September 28, 1985, he and Dorothy had an argument that turned violent. Dorothy not only admitted having sexual relations with Kelly's boyfriend, said Leonard, but said she wanted her husband to move out so that she could continue to have an affair with Albright. "Craig's not leaving, you are," Leonard said his wife yelled. "I don't love you anymore. You're a wimp, you're a punk, you're not a man, you don't satisfy me."

She then grabbed a steak knife and lunged at him, said Tyburski, whereupon he "exploded," grabbed her, bashed her head several times into a beam near the basement stairs, and flung her into the freezer.

In a state of shock, Leonard calmly walked upstairs and washed his hands. Thirty minutes later he returned, closed the freezer lid, and locked Dorothy in her icy tomb because, "I loved her and didn't want to part with her."

Leonard was charged with second-degree murder, tried, convicted, and sentenced to a 20- to 40-year prison term.

And Kelly and her mother finally rest in peace.

WELCOME TO MY NIGHTMARE

Earl Keys was happy to see the light finally filter through the bedroom curtains of his Detroit home on a January 1949 morning. A few hours before, the auto factory worker had awakened from the most vivid, frightening nightmare of his life. He hadn't been able to go back to sleep and had tossed and turned, waiting for morning to arrive.

As he ate breakfast with his wife, he told her about the dream. He and another man, whom he did not know, were walking through a cemetery together. Suddenly, two graves opened up, and a ghost rose out of each. As the spirits approached, Earl was stunned to see that one was a vision of himself and the other was that of the stranger who walked with him.

Even worse, Earl realized that his ghost was neither friendly nor benevolent. The apparition, in fact, wanted to fight him, and if Earl lost, it would be he who would have to enter the grave. Earl's unknown comrade faced the same situation. But as often happens with nightmares, Earl was frightened awake before he had to enter into the macabre battle.

Having finished telling his story, Earl kissed his wife goodbye and headed to his car to go to work. The car wouldn't start. Earl tightened his lips and shook his head. The day seemed to be picking up where his night had left off. Now he'd have to take the bus, which meant he'd be late for work.

The vivid specters from his dream still haunted Earl, and he stared vacantly out the window of the bus as it lumbered through the streets. For several minutes he didn't notice that another rider had sat down next to him. When Earl did realize that the seat next to him was occupied, he turned to the stranger and asked if he knew what time the bus arrived at his factory, the Hudson Body Company.

The man, Woody Collins, said that he too worked at Hudson but, no, he wasn't familiar with the bus schedule. "I haven't ridden the bus to work for two years," he said. "And I wouldn't this morning, except my car didn't start."

"No kidding," said Earl as he chuckled almost imperceptibly. "That's why I'm here. Mine wouldn't start either, and it was really irritating because I only got a couple of hours of sleep last night."

"Me too," replied Woody. "I had a terrible, bizarre nightmare."

Incredulous, Earl then listened as Woody described, detail for detail, a dream exactly the same as his. The only difference — Earl was the stranger in Woody's dream, and Woody was the stranger in Earl's.

Earl then shocked Woody by telling him they had walked together in separate but identical nightmares. The two men struggled to find a reason or explanation. But the only thin threads of reality that connected them were that both worked for the same company and, they discovered, both were born in the same county in Kentucky.

When they stepped off the bus, their unusual association ended. They never met again, either while awake or dreaming.

DRIFTING OFF TO DEATH

Al Davis pursed his lips and shook his head slowly as he read the story in his November 28, 1951 morning newspaper. During a heavy snowstorm the day before, several Kalamazoo College students had seen one of their classmates, Carolyn Drown, step into a car occupied by two unidentified young men. The 18-year-old woman had not been seen or heard from since, and her parents and the police feared the worst.

Davis, a 61-year-old farmer/woodsman, was glad that he lived in the small community of Walhalla, in the northwest part of the Lower Peninsula, where he didn't have to worry about such "big city" problems. His biggest concern that day was to prepare for the arrival of a pair of hunters from the Kalamazoo area. Roy Lee Olson and Valorus Matthies had paid to stay in a small cabin at the back of Davis' property and had hired him as a guide.

The two men, both 22 years old, arrived early that evening, and their cocky attitude and boisterous behavior immediately irritated Davis. Davis' dog, too, seemed bothered by both the men and their car. The agitated animal circled Olson and Matthies and their vehicle several times while intently sniffing. When Olson kicked at the dog, Davis said and did nothing.

But when the young men blurted out their desire to seduce a 13-year-old local girl they had seen, Davis interrupted. Slowly and coldly he warned them that if they so much as talked to the girl, he would personally wrap wire around their necks and drag them back to Kalamazoo behind his car. Davis left no doubt that he meant what he said, and the men instantly shut up and headed for the cabin.

That night Al Davis had a strange, vivid dream. Carolyn Drown, the missing co-ed, had been murdered, and Davis watched as her faceless killers, two of them, threw her body into a snowdrift along a lonely road. Davis stared at Drown's body until it was rapidly covered by the heavy snowfall, and then he looked up. Looming over the site were two huge trees, and in the distance across a cornfield stood a lone house.

Davis awoke before sunrise and reluctantly went out to get Olson and Matthies for the day's hunt. When he got to the cabin, however, he was surprised to discover that the men and their gear were gone.

Davis figured he'd probably scared them off, but as far as he was concerned it was good riddance. What bothered him more, at the moment, were the stark visions that remained from his sleep. Never before had he had a dream that seemed so real.

For the next several days, Davis carefully followed newspaper articles about the investigation into Carolyn Drown's disappearance. Police had little to go on, said the reports. The witnesses who had seen Drown get into a car could only say that the vehicle was a common model and color. No one could come up with even a partial license plate number, and no one had gotten a good look at the men inside. When, by the end of the week, Davis realized the police were desperate for *any* kind of lead, he overcame his embarrassment and called to tell them about his strange dream.

Investigators, figuring they had nothing to lose but a little time, brought Davis down to Kalamazoo and drove him over miles of the area's look-alike country roads. After several hours of fruitless searching, Davis and his State Police driver returned to headquarters for a coffee break. As Davis apologized for apparently wasting the officer's time, another trooper just coming on duty said he thought he knew a place with the landmarks Davis had seen in his dream.

The trooper and Davis headed to the area, not far from Vicksburg. Shortly after they turned onto a seldom-traveled dirt road, Davis blurted, "There it is. That's the cornfield, and there's the house." A few blocks farther they stopped near a mound of snow under a pair of towering oaks. After a few minutes of digging and sweeping, the policeman uncovered a body. It was Carolyn Drown's.

Police didn't spend any time pondering the unbelievability of what had just happened. No matter the reason, Al Davis had been right once, so maybe he could tell them more. Besides his prophetic dream, police asked, had he seen, heard or even thought of anything else out of the ordinary in the days since he first read about Carolyn Drown? Davis reminded them that his life in Walhalla was pretty routine and that the only other excitement he'd had lately was his confrontation with the two hunters. And, oh yes, it did strike him as odd that something about the men's car had caused his dog to get unusually excited.

Police checked drivers license records and discovered that both Roy Olson and Valorus Matthies lived not far from where Carolyn

Drown's body was uncovered. When authorities went to question the men, they found that Olson's car was the same model and color as the one Carolyn Drown had gotten into before her disappearance. A subsequent thorough examination of the vehicle turned up hair and other evidence that later convinced a jury to convict Olson and Matthies of Carolyn Drown's murder. They were sentenced to life imprisonment.

Al Davis returned to Walhalla where he lived out the rest of his life uneventfully. He never had another dream worth telling, and he wondered to his dying day why his sleep had once taken him to a place he'd never seen to help solve the murder of a young woman he'd never met.

FROM DREAMS TO RICHES

November 21, 1987, ended pretty much like any other Saturday for 68-year-old Joseph Polachek and his wife, Marguerite. The couple watched television at their Owosso home, then went to bed. And as on previous Saturday nights, the Polacheks flipped the channel to avoid watching the live Michigan Super Lotto jackpot drawing and later news reports of the winning numbers.

It wasn't that the Polacheks weren't interested in the lottery. On the contrary, Joseph, a retiree from the Buick plant in Flint, was an avid player and bought several tickets for the Saturday night Super Lotto drawing each week.

And though he was sure he would win one day, he didn't seem anxious to find out. Perhaps it was superstition or habit, but Polachek did not like to see the winning numbers broadcast on TV. He much preferred to lay out all of his tickets on the kitchen table on Sunday morning and, while drinking his coffee, compare them to the winning numbers printed in the newspaper.

While getting dressed the next morning, Joseph told Marguerite about a strange dream he had had during the night. In the dream, according to *Money For Nothing: Stories of Michigan's Million-Dollar Lottery Winners* (Friede Publications, 1988), Polachek was holding all of his lottery tickets in his hands while talking with his brother. When he glanced down at the tickets, one particular set of numbers suddenly stood out. "I won," Polachek exclaimed. "I've got the winning numbers." But he added, "I'm having a hard time getting the money." Polachek awoke but remembered which set of numbers he had dreamed were the winners.

When he checked the Sunday newspaper, he found out not only was he the winner of $3.8 million, but also that he had correctly dreamed which six numbers had scored for him.

On Monday morning the Polacheks phoned the Lottery Bureau in Lansing, made an appointment, then later drove to the capital city to pick up $191,433, the first installment of their prize. Shortly after they arrived, their ticket was confirmed as a winner and they filled out the required forms and applications. Then, for reasons never explained, lottery officials told them they couldn't collect their money that day after all. They would have to come back the next day.

Polacheck was annoyed, but once the check was in his hands he didn't ask or care why the rest of his dream had become reality — why he had had a difficult time collecting the money.

GOING HOME

Mabel Schneider felt the beginnings of the fear that gnaws at a parent when a child is late arriving home. It was 11:20 a.m., past the time on January 12, 1928, when her five-year-old daughter should have come home from kindergarten for lunch. From the window of her Mt. Morris home, Mrs. Schneider could see far down the snow-packed route Dorothy normally walked. The little blond-haired girl was nowhere in sight.

Ten minutes later Mrs. Schneider started walking toward the village school, hoping to meet Dorothy on the way. About halfway there she stopped at a gas station and asked the proprietor's wife, whom she knew, if she had seen Dorothy. Yes, said the woman, the little girl had passed by at about the same time that she usually did on her way home. Somewhere between the gas station and home, Dorothy had disappeared.

Now frantic, Mrs. Schneider ran to the school and blurted out the frightening situation to Dorothy's teacher. The teacher immediately phoned the school superintendent, who in turn contacted the Genesee County Sheriff's Department. Deputies picked up Leslie Schneider, Mabel's husband and Dorothy's father, at work and told him about his daughter's apparent disappearance as they drove him home.

At about 1 p.m. sheriff's deputies, school personnel, and the Schneiders fanned out in the area between the service station and the Schneiders' house. Finding no sign of the little girl or no one else who had seen her, the deputies began driving the area's main roads, looking for Dorothy or signs of anything unusual.

At 3 p.m., roughly three miles west of the gas station where Dorothy was last seen, a deputy looked down a muddy side road and saw a spot where a car had obviously been stuck. When the officer checked, he discovered a man's footprints leading through the snow on the road shoulder to a fence. On the other side of the fence, the tiny imprints of a child's overshoes joined the adult tracks. The trail crossed a large field to a wooded ravine that dropped to a creek. Not far into the wooded area, the deputy found Dorothy's cap, coat and sweater.

The deputy rushed to a nearby farmhouse, owned by Archie Bacon, and phoned headquarters for help. Soon, carloads of other officers arrived and combed the area, and at 5:30 p.m. searchers made a grisly discovery. Dorothy Schneider had been killed and her tiny body carved into several pieces and thrown into the creek. A subsequent autopsy determined that she had been sexually assaulted before being stabbed to death and then mutilated.

When Dorothy's killer returned to his car and tried to drive away, however, the vehicle became stuck in heavy mud. The slayer was forced to walk to Bacon's farmhouse and ask for help. Bacon, unaware of what had happened in the woods, helped the nervous man extricate his vehicle, an old robin's-egg-blue Dodge sedan, from the mire.

Bacon told investigators the man was about 50 years old and approximately 5 feet, 9 inches tall. Though Bacon said he had never met the man before, he was positive he would recognize him if he saw him again.

What seemed to be a sweet lead quickly soured. Authorities were convinced that Dorothy's killer was someone local who knew the area fairly well. So, using Michigan Secretary of State Office records, authorities compiled a lengthy list of all the owners of "old" four-door Dodges within a 50-mile radius of Mt. Morris. The police would have to check the vehicles out one at a time to find out which were light blue, a very common color. They would then have to determine if any 50-year-old males drove the cars and bring each in for possible identification by Bacon. The process could take years, with no guarantee the killer and Bacon would again stand face to face. Nevertheless, investigators began the near-impossible task.

But they also tried short cuts. Pursuit planes flew over Genesee and surrounding counties searching for abandoned automobiles, and roadblocks were set up on all routes into and out of the greater Flint area. Bacon flipped through more than 150 "mug shots" of known sex offenders, and police brought in for questioning several men in the area with known criminal pasts. Bacon recognized no one in the photographs, and the 50-60 suspects picked up by police were all exonerated.

Four days after the killing, when both tips and investigators were near exhausted, the police got an unexpected — and, as it turned out, unexplainable — break.

The morning of January 16, the day of Dorothy Schneider's funeral, Harold Lotridge's alarm clock interrupted a vivid nightmare. In his sleep he had seen a man — a man he knew well — carrying Dorothy Schneider, while the little girl repeatedly cried, "I want to go home."

Twenty-four-year-old Lotridge, who lived in Owosso, 30 miles southwest of Mt. Morris, fought the overpowering feeling that the man he saw in his nightmare was the killer. It just couldn't be, he kept telling himself. The man in the dream, 47-year-old Adolph Hotelling, was a classic "pillar of the community," a respected and respectable family man with children of his own, including a daughter about the age of Dorothy Schneider. Hotelling, a deacon in the Owosso Church of Christ, was an ultradevout man who seemed dedicated to his family and church. Lotridge attended the same church and just the night before had participated in a communion service over which Hotelling had presided.

Young Lotridge, a carpenter, reported for work as usual to a job site in Flushing, a small community northwest of Flint. His father, John, was also a carpenter and worked at the same project, a new school building. As they pounded and sawed, Harold told his father about the strange dream that had left him with the untenable conviction that Adolph Hotelling was Dorothy Schneider's slayer. The elder Lotridge agreed that it was unbelievable and advised his son to forget it. Any further mention, he said, would probably needlessly damage Hotelling's impeccable reputation. Anger, fear and a lynch-mob atmosphere, as both Lotridges knew, had already caused some ugly incidents involving other suspects.

A coworker, however, overheard their conversation and, taking a long shot at an $8,000 reward that had been posted, went straight to the police. It was a strange tale, but authorities at that point were desperate enough to investigate any lead. Besides, when they checked their master list of owners of Dodge sedans, they discovered Adolph Hotelling's name, which because of his reputation had been moved to the bottom as a "least likely" suspect. In one trip west of Flint, figured investigators, they could squelch the Lotridge dream story and scratch Hotelling's name off the car-suspect list.

Sheriff's deputies confronted a surprised Harold Lotridge at the Flushing job site, and he reluctantly repeated the details of his dream. The officers then drove to Hotelling's Owosso-area home. A relaxed Hotelling greeted them and, when asked about his old Dodge, offered without hesitation to show them the vehicle. Officers went to an outbuilding and found a beat-up old car but with a shiny, new-looking black finish. When one deputy reached to grab a door handle to look inside, his large signet ring accidentally scratched the metal. Fresh black paint stuck to the ring, and the scratch revealed a robin's-egg-blue undercoat.

In the days before warrants were a necessity, the officers searched the property further and found clothes identical to those Archie Bacon had said the man in the stuck car had worn. In a pocket of a gray overcoat was a blood-stained, double-edged knife.

The officers arrested Hotelling and took him to Flint where, after being positively identified by Archie Bacon, he confessed to the murder of Dorothy Schneider, repeatedly saying, "I don't know why I did it."

Hotelling was subsequently tried and sentenced to life in prison.

He died in Marquette prison in 1955. Had it not been for Harold Lotridge's unexplainable dream, Adolph Hotelling might have remained free to cause more nightmares.

GHOSTS

Although not everyone believes in ghosts, just about everyone enjoys a good ghost story.

Ghost stories have long been staples of fact, fiction and folklore mainly because people have always wondered what, if anything, happens to us after we die. In fact, throughout most of recorded history, the reality of ghosts has been accepted without question. Virtually all cultures have believed at one time or another that spirits of the dead are able to return to the world of the living, either in visible or sensory form. Only Western science and religion — and only in the past couple of hundred years — have raised doubts and preached outright disbelief.

Accompanying or perhaps in reaction to the skepticism, however, came study and investigation. During the past century, several dozen serious researchers have made attempts to find out whether ghosts really exist and, if so, what it is they are.

It has been almost impossible, however, to gather hard, scientific-type data on something that, if it exists at all, doesn't conform to quantifiable, measurable physical laws. "Evidence," then, has been largely anecdotal. That is, researchers talk to people who claim they have experienced ghosts and then try to determine the veracity of the stories. Serious investigators eventually dismiss as many as 98 percent of alleged ghostly encounters as being unbelievable, faked or having provable natural causes.

The few remaining cases, however, cannot be explained in any rational, scientific way. As a result, most parapsychological researchers have concluded that something non-physical does remain after our physical bodies die.

Unfortunately they haven't had much success in determining or defining exactly what it is. General, vague descriptions speak of "spirits of the dead that exist in some other sphere of existence," "manifestations of persistent personal energy," "psychic remnants of past events," or simply, "survival phenomena." There is no consensus on whether ghosts have intelligence or personality or are even aware of their own existence.

While there may be little agreement among researchers as to what ghosts are, they do pretty much concur on how ghosts behave. First, ghosts do not physically harm humans, say just about all paranormal experts. And second, whatever natural laws govern the unnatural existence of ghosts evidently restrict how they can interact with the living. About the only ways they make their presence known is by mysterious noises, unusual smells, cold breezes, movements of objects, and occasionally becoming temporarily visible.

Michigan residents have experienced their fair share of ghostly manifestations. The past three centuries have produced hundreds of strange tales that embrace fact, legend, folklore and the apocryphal. No matter their origin, Michigan ghosts, like all others, turn out to be basically harmless and behave in somewhat limited ways. As a result, the large collection of Michigan ghost stories quickly becomes redundant.

What follows is a small but fascinating cross section of reports of encounters between the Michigan living and spirits of the Michigan dead. They range from eerie accounts by rational, sane, believable people to entertaining campfire ghost stories. It's not always easy, however, to determine which is which.

JUST DYING TO GET UP

You would think that dying would be a sure way to break an old habit. For one man, however, even death apparently doesn't stop him from beginning his daily routine.

A part-time policewoman found that out in 1981, shortly after moving into a 130-year-old Rochester farmhouse she had purchased. The woman, who had fallen asleep on the couch, was awakened at

4:30 a.m. by the sound of a door slamming. As she sat up, she experienced an inner cold and felt what she described as a "presence."

The incidents have continued regularly and without variation since. Every morning at 4:30, the woman hears somebody walking, then a door slams. In the spring and summer, the noise comes from the large, padlocked front door, and in the fall and winter, from a solid side door, also locked. One night before going to bed, she applied duct tape to the crack between the side door and molding. The next morning the duct-tape seal was broken.

The ghost occasionally left the front door open, which during early spring caused the house to get cold. So one night the homeowner stuck a note to the front door that read, "Dear Ghost: Please close the door when you go out, as it's very cold outside." The door hasn't been left open since.

In 1991 Dr. Richard Brooks, chairman of Oakland University's philosophy department, visited the farmhouse in the company of a *Detroit News* reporter. Dr. Brooks, who seriously studies ghostly phenomenon (see p. 88), speculated that the Rochester woman was witnessing the "psychic corpse" of a farmer who once lived in the house. The man had probably spent his entire adult life leaving the house at 4:30 a.m. to work, perhaps in the big red barn still standing not far away. The habit was probably so deeply ingrained, said Dr. Brooks, that his spirit has continued the early morning exits.

Because there are no other problems, the policewoman who owns the cozy old farmhouse has no plans to leave. "I've learned to live with it," she says.

THE HORRIBLE HAG OF MARTIN STREET

When Bill and Lillian Adams walked through the old, weathered house they were considering renting, they didn't go into the tiny, dark room off the kitchen. They liked what they saw of the rest of the $1^{1}/_{2}$-story frame dwelling and immediately signed a rental agreement. A week later, in late fall 1961, the Adams and their five young children settled into the home, on Martin Street in a quiet, though declining neighborhood on Detroit's west side.

Shortly after moving in, Bill, who worked nights, discovered that the back room they had only glanced at was an ideal place for him to sleep during the day. Although it had barely enough floor space for a bed, it was dark, even during the day. The cloudy, dirty glass of a single small casement window high up on the back wall allowed only a few diffuse patches of light to reach the drab, blue-green walls. And it was quiet. Because the room was built as a near-private addition off the rear of the house, Bill was separated from the noise of his playing children.

At first Bill didn't notice there was another reason he was rarely disturbed. His children and the family's pet terrier seemed to sense something about the room that made them avoid it. They never stepped inside, even when Bill wasn't there.

About six months after moving in, Bill, too, began feeling a vague, inexplicable uneasiness about the room. He had trouble falling asleep there, and then suffered nightmares so horrible they "left me limp with fear," he said. In one dream he opened a door and a mutilated body fell out. Many other dreams ended with him sitting up in bed screaming. Adams, who had never been bothered by nightmares before, eventually moved into the main bedroom, where he rested peacefully.

Bill and Lillian avoided talking about the back room and its mysterious effect on Bill. They especially didn't say anything to Adams' grandmother when she volunteered to sleep there during an August 1962 visit from Atlanta. After her first night in the room, Adams' grandmother came to the breakfast table visibly shaken. All night, she said, she had been kept awake by frightening sounds, like someone was trying to get in. She said she wouldn't sleep there again and then cut short her stay and hurried back to Georgia.

Two months later the Adams hosted another relative from Georgia, a cousin by marriage named (Mr.) Shirley Patterson. Patterson had come to Detroit to buy a car, stay a couple of days, and then drive the vehicle back home to Decatur. Again, Bill and Lillian said nothing about the back room other than to tell Patterson that he could sleep there.

On Saturday, October 27, Patterson entered the back bedroom at 11:30 p.m., shortly after Bill had left for work. Lillian was in the bathroom setting her freshly washed hair in curlers. Patterson stripped to his underwear, clicked off the ceiling light, climbed into bed, and turned to face the wall.

Moments later he felt something roll him back over. As his eyes adjusted to the near-darkness, he saw a shape standing just outside the bedroom doorway. It was a woman with long hair and wearing a short fur coat over a blue dress. She faced away from Patterson, but he knew it wasn't Lillian. He jumped out of bed and, while screaming for Lillian to come, ran toward the figure. At that instant, lights that were on in the house went out.

Seconds later Patterson and Lillian met in the kitchen, and the lights came back on. From the back room came a crying groan — described by Patterson and Lillian as part human, part animal — followed by a thick, rotten smell that made them both feel ill.

When Patterson described what he had seen to Lillian, she ran to a closet and returned with a fur coat and blue dress she owned. The clothes, identical to what Patterson said the figure was wearing, wreaked with the same revolting odor.

Lillian and Patterson waited up until Bill Adams came home from work Sunday morning and then told him what had happened. Adams called the police, who searched the house thoroughly. Though they could still slightly detect the smell, they found nothing that might have caused it.

Bill Adams had had enough. He was a stable, reasonable man who didn't believe in anything like ghosts or the supernatural. But he did know something very strange was going on in the back bedroom, and he decided he would stay there every night until he found out what.

It didn't take long.

That same Sunday night about 7:30, Bill Adams went into the silent, dark room and lay on his side on the bed. Very soon he had the uneasy feeling that somebody — or some thing — was in the room with him. He slowly rolled over to look, then froze in stark terror as his eyes met the hideous face of a formless hag only inches from his. Its macabre eyes stared through long, stringy, brittle, gray hair. Its drooling mouth moved as if to talk, but all that came out was a hiss and a sickening stench.

Adams ran screaming from the bed. When he reached the front room, he was so hysterical that Patterson had to wrestle him into a chair. As Patterson and Lillian wrapped Adams with a blanket and tried to calm him, the overpowering smell drifted through the house.

Grabbing their children, Bill and Lillian ran to the neighbors, where they called the police. Again officers searched their house. And again they detected nothing but faint whiffs of the terrible odor.

The Adams family spent the rest of the night at their neighbor's home, and the next morning they moved in with Lillian's parents, who lived in Dearborn. The following week Adams — during the day and in the company of friends and relatives — returned and hauled out all the family's belongings.

That same week a *Detroit Free Press* story about the Adamses' experiences attracted so many curiosity seekers to the house that police had to post an around-the-clock guard. In the following weeks and months, the house's owner was inundated by requests and monetary offers from persons who wanted to spend nights or weekends there. Even electronics engineers from a Big Three automaker reportedly sought the owner's permission to wire the bedroom with special detection equipment. But the owner refused to let anybody but the police inside.

When the notoriety finally subsided, the landlord rented the dwelling to others, who lived there without incident.

"THEY KILT ME"

"Who lit a candle?" wondered Isaac Van Woert. "There's no one inside."

It was 8 p.m., September 27, 1845, only two days after Isaac and his family had moved into a vacant house in Dixboro, near Ann Arbor, after traveling by covered wagon from the state of New York. Mrs. Van Woert had walked down the road to introduce herself to the neighbors, and the two young Van Woert boys were exploring their back yard. Isaac had stepped out into the front yard and was casually combing his hair when a dim light from inside the house interrupted the darkness.

Puzzled, Isaac walked to the front window, cupped his hands to his face, and peered inside. Standing in the living room was a woman holding a lit candle in her left hand. Her right hand clutched her dress and apron near her waist, and she stooped slightly forward. A white cloth wrapped around her head accented her large, sunken eyes. Her mouth formed the grin of death that appears on corpses as rigor mortis sets in — pale lips pulled back taut to slightly expose her teeth.

The woman shuffled across the floor, entered the bedroom and closed the door. Isaac went into the house, walked quietly across the living room to the bedroom, and opened the door. It was dark, so he lit a candle and stepped inside. He was alone in the room.

Thinking the long wagon ride from New York had probably exhausted him to the point of causing the apparition, Isaac said nothing to his family about his strange experience.

He did, however, make some casual inquiries among the townspeople about the house and found out that a widow named Martha Mulholland and her 15-year-old son, Joseph, had been the previous residents. Less than a month before the Van Woerts' arrival, Martha had died, suddenly and unexpectedly, in the house. Isaac asked what Martha looked like. Her description matched the woman he had seen through the house window.

How, wondered Isaac, could he have imagined seeing the exact likeness of a woman he had never met, had never even heard of, and who was in fact dead? He had the unsettling feeling that perhaps what he had seen was somehow real. Over the next month and a half, not only was his suspicion confirmed, but also he learned the reason why Martha Mulholland could not rest in peace.

Nearly two weeks passed before Isaac had a second encounter with Martha's spirit. In the middle of a cool early October night, Isaac got up from bed and opened the bedroom door on his way to the outhouse. Though it was an overcast, moonless night, the living room was light. And standing only five feet from him was Martha Mulholland.

Instinctively, Isaac stepped back while saying, "What do you want?"

"He has robbed me. He got it little by little, until they kilt me," replied Martha in a heavy Irish accent. "Now he has got it all."

"Who has it all?" asked Isaac.

"James. James. Yes, James has got it at last, but it won't do him long," said Martha. Then the room went dark, and Isaac was alone again.

The next day Isaac found out that Martha had a brother-in-law named James Mulholland. Gossip around Dixboro had it that, after Martha's husband's death, James had swindled money and property from her. Some townspeople whispered that they thought James may have even had a hand in Martha's sudden illness and death. James still lived in the area and, in fact, had taken Martha's son, Joseph, into his home after her death.

At night a week later, Isaac awoke when his bedroom was suddenly filled with a light that did not wake his wife. Standing at the foot of the bed was Martha, who said, "James can't hurt me any more. No, he can't. I am out of his reach. But why don't they get Joseph away? Oh, my boy. Why not come away?" The room then went dark, as though someone had blown out a candle.

The next night at about 11, Isaac was relaxing, feet propped up on the stove hearth, after his family had gone to bed. Suddenly, the door opened and a man entered, carrying Martha in his arms. "She is dying. She will die," he said, and then dissolved into the night air while the door closed without a noise.

Shortly after sunrise the following morning, Isaac, a carpenter, left the house to go to work. Appearing in the front yard for only a few seconds was Martha, who blurted, "I fear something will befall my boy."

The sixth time Isaac saw Martha was a week later, when at midnight the bedroom again suddenly became light. Isaac looked at his wife to see if she, too, would awaken, but Martha, standing at the foot of the bed, raised her hand and said, "She will not."

Martha then leaned forward suddenly, as though in great pain. Her right hand pressed hard against her stomach, and her left hand held up a vial of liquid. "The doctor said it was Balm of Gilead," she groaned, then faded from sight.

Isaac still said nothing to his family or anyone else about his strange encounters. He wasn't particularly frightened by Martha's spirit, which seemed harmless. More than anything he was frustrated that he didn't know how to respond to what he felt were her underlying pleas for help.

Perhaps sensing Isaac's frustration, Martha became more direct. As Isaac puttered at a workbench one evening, Martha again appeared and moaned, "Oh, they kilt me. They kilt me."

"Who killed you?" asked Isaac.

"I will show you," said Martha, who then led Isaac out the back door. Standing near the backyard fence were two men, who looked downcast and dejected. One was James Mulholland. The other Isaac recognized as a peddler who regularly visited the area and had recently passed through selling herbs and patent medicines. As Isaac watched, the two men melted from sight and disappeared in a blue haze. He turned to look back at Martha, but she, too, was gone.

Not long after, however, she reappeared and said to Isaac, "I want you to tell James to repent. Oh, if he would repent! But he won't, he can't."

Isaac asked if he should report the two men who had killed her to the authorities. "There will be a time," she replied. "The time will come."

But, evidently, even Martha grew impatient. At midnight on November 6, 1845, less than two months after Isaac had moved into the house, Martha again appeared in his bedroom. This time, however, she stood erect, not stooped, and at the side, not the foot, of the bed. She appeared angry, even menacing. Instead of keeping the five-foot distance she had during all other meetings, she leaned into Isaac's face and hissed, "I don't want anybody here. I wanted to tell you a secret, and I thought I had. I don't want anybody here."

The next morning Isaac moved his family and belongings out of the house. He also went to Justice of the Peace William Perry, at Ann Arbor, who took an official deposition of the details of Isaac's encounters with Martha Mulholland's apparition.

When the deposition was made public in several newspapers, Dixboro residents demanded that Martha's body be disinterred and an autopsy performed. Her body was exhumed, and a coroner's inquest determined that she had, in fact, died from poison "administered by a person unknown."

There were strong suspicions that James Mulholland — with the help of the traveling herb peddler, who pretended to be a doctor — had murdered Martha. But in the absence of proof, the unusual incident faded from importance as all participants renewed their own struggles with life in frontier Michigan.

DO NOT DISTURB

During the fall of 1980, reports came out of Westland that several motorists had seen a very attractive female spectre standing in the middle of Henry Ruff Road, near Butler Cemetery. A few drivers had been so startled by the sight of the ephemeral woman — with long blonde hair and dressed in a flowing white gown — that they lost control of their vehicles and went into the ditch.

When word of the incidents reached Marion Kuclo — also known as Gundella, a "good" witch from Garden City — she went to investigate. While wandering though a remote, neglected area of the old cemetery, Kuclo discovered a grave washed open by heavy rains. Exposed at the bottom of the burial site were pieces of a wood casket and human bones that had been scattered by animals. Stuck to some of the boards were bits of tattered silk, and the skeleton was that of a female with long, strawberry-blond hair. The tombstone at the disturbed grave was so old that the only part of the inscription Kuclo could read was the name, "Alice."

Soon after, Alice's remains were reinterred and her grave again filled in. Evidently satisfied that her eternal resting place was restored, Alice again lay in peace. No more sightings were reported.

GUESS WHAT'S COMING TO DINNER?

When you sit down at a fine restaurant, you certainly don't expect a ghost to interrupt your meal. But if you dine at the Bowers Harbor Inn, near Traverse City, you could be distracted by a poltergeist that has been a pain in the palate for more than 30 years.

The inn was built around the turn of the century by J. W. Stickney, a wealthy businessman from Chicago. Stickney and his wife, Genevive, used the mansion — set amidst stately oaks and majestic pines on the picturesque Old Mission Peninsula — as their summer home.

Genevive enjoyed the good life and it showed. She was quite large. She didn't like the way she looked but was not about to cut calories or exert any extra physical effort to lose pounds. Instead, she ordered a specially made gilt-edged mirror whose reflection made her appear much thinner. Her weight problem was solved, at least in her eyes.

But evidently not in her husband's. Without Genevive's knowledge he carried on a long-time affair with his secretary.

As the Stickneys aged, they found it difficult to climb the two-story mansion's stairs and so had an elevator installed. Not long after, J.W. became ill and entered a Chicago hospital, where he died. It was then that Genevive finally discovered her husband's affair. J.W. Stickney had named his mistress as the beneficiary of his estate. Devastated, Genevive returned to the mansion and, according to most accounts, hanged herself in the elevator shaft.

She was dead, but she didn't leave, say subsequent owners.

Jim and Fern Bryant, for instance, began experiencing strange goings-on shortly after they bought the mansion in 1959 and turned it into a restaurant. Mirrors fell from the walls in unoccupied rooms, they said, and lights suddenly turned on and off, with switches changing position as well. Toni Scharing and Bruce and Sally Jidge bought the place in 1964 and lived upstairs while continuing to operate the lower level as a restaurant. They told stories of the elevator running on its own and securely locked doors flying open.

Employees of Shelde Enterprises, which bought the restaurant in 1974 and has run it since, say the occasional antics of what they, too, believe to be Genevive's ghost are annoying and disruptive but basically harmless. One long-term senior manager said that, one evening as he left after closing up the lounge area, a fan behind the bar turned on, apparently by itself. He shut the fan off and turned to leave. Again, the fan began turning. Again he shut it off and left. But when he came back to check moments later, he found the fan running again. He shut it off a third time, and it finally stayed off. Another time two cooks routinely chopped onions on a counter beneath a rack of pots and pans. Suddenly, a 2-quart saucepan flew sideways off its holder and crashed into the sink, six feet away.

The inn's staff aren't the only ones who have encountered Genevive. In the busy dining area one evening, Genevive tossed the salad — literally. With no person standing near the salad bar, a bowl of greens suddenly flew up from the table and through the air — patrons said as though deliberately thrown by an unseen hand — and crashed on the floor.

53

Another night a woman who was the last patron to leave the restaurant went upstairs to the restroom while her husband got their car. The women's lounge consists of two rooms: a sitting area, which was formerly Genevive's bedroom, and an adjoining bathroom. The bathroom is small, with only two stalls and a pedestal sink. The woman, alone in the lounge area, went into the bathroom, closed the door, and entered a stall. Suddenly, a roll of tissue rolled across the floor under the stall door and up against her foot. A second roll quickly followed. As the woman fled from the restroom, she noted there still was no other person around.

On another occasion a young woman, obviously upset, rushed downstairs from the lounge. She blurted to her dinner companions that while primping in front of Genevive's gilt-edged mirror, now equipped with standard glass, the reflection of another woman had appeared. The second woman, hair pulled back tightly into a bun, stared into the glass directly over the patron's shoulder. The startled patron spun quickly around, but no one was there. The description of the face in the mysterious reflection, said long-time employees, matched tintype pictures of Genevive Stickney they had seen.

Bowers Harbor Inn staffers are not only familiar with Genevive, they're also comfortable with her spirit. At closing time late one night, a manager and an assistant — the last two people in the building — turned off the light in the women's restroom and headed downstairs together. They hadn't yet reached the bottom when they heard a strange hissing coming from the room they had just checked and closed. They returned upstairs and opened the bathroom door to find the sink faucet turned on full force. The manager sighed, turned it off, and again left after saying, "Good night, Genevive."

LIGHTHOUSE GHOSTS

More than a hundred lighthouses are spaced around Michigan's 3,000-plus miles of Great Lakes coastline. Many of the colorful, historic structures have stood for a century or longer, and the beacons from 64 still mark safe harbors and warn mariners of points, shoals and other dangerous areas.

Through the turn of the 20th century, lighthouses had "keepers," who climbed the towers to light wicks or lamps at sundown and to extinguish them at sunrise. During the shipping season, in fact, lighthouses were homes to the keepers and sometimes their families. But beginning in the 1920s, the tenders of the lights began losing their jobs to technology. As automated lenses were installed, one by one the lighthouse keepers moved out.

The spirits of a few, however, may have stuck around, according to some reports.

Several Coast Guardsmen, for instance, have claimed they were bothered by mysterious happenings while stationed at the Eagle Harbor Lighthouse on Lake Superior during the 1960s and 70s. According to both enlisted men and officers, doors opened and closed on their own, furniture got moved, dresser drawers were pulled out and crashed to the floor, and with the dead of night often came the sounds of rattling chains, faraway voices and other strange noises.

The servicemen blamed the nuisances on the ghost of a grouchy old lightkeeper they named "George." Since 1851 several lighthouses have stood at the tip of the rocky point that marks the entrance to Eagle Harbor. On three separate occasions, the various structures were tended by keepers named George, and local residents say that one of them is buried in a nearby cemetery.

George evidently prefers the sound of Lake Superior waves lapping the shore of the Keewenaw Peninsula to modern music. "I know for a fact that George hates rock music," says one Seaman, "because when the music gets too loud, he turns my stereo off and ejects tapes from the player."

Ghosts haunt two other lighthouses in Michigan waters, according to Charles K. Hyde, author of *The Northern Lights: Lighthouses of the Upper Great Lakes* (Two Peninsula Press, 1986).

The spirit of John Herman, for instance, pestered keepers at Waugoshance Shoal, near the Straits of Mackinac, from 1894 until the lighthouse closed in 1912. Herman, who became keeper of the Waugoshance Light in 1885, loved to do two things to break up the monotony of his assignment, says Hyde. He drank and he played practical jokes.

One evening in August 1894, Herman's pastimes led to quite unexpected consequences. As an assistant lit the lantern, Herman locked the man in the lamp room. While the assistant shouted, Herman went outside and, laughing loudly, staggered down a pier. When the assistant finally freed himself, he discovered that Herman had disappeared, presumably having fallen off the pier and drowned.

But according to lighthouse lore, Herman's spirited spirit continued to fool around at Waugoshance. Keepers who fell asleep while on duty had their chairs kicked out from under them. Others reported suffering the same annoyance as Herman's assistant, getting locked in the tower or other rooms. And at times when no person was around to do it, coal was mysteriously shoveled into the boilers. The incidents continued until the lighthouse was closed and abandoned.

At the New Presque Isle Light, built in 1870 on Lake Huron north of Alpena, the ghost of a lightkeeper's wife cries and moans. According to the story passed along by Hyde, the lightkeeper would regularly lock his wife in the tower and then set off to visit a girlfriend in a nearby town. Not surprisingly the keeper's wife vehemently protested the situation. So the keeper murdered her, figuring that he could then continue his love affair in peace.

But, according to the legend, even that didn't end his wife's complaining. Her spirit returned to the tower and tormented her husband and others who have lived there with her wailing.

THE REUNION

One of the strangest incidents of America's Civil War involved a Michigan infantry unit and its drummer boy, John Downey, from Three Rivers. What happened was so unbelievable that Downey, afraid he would be ridiculed or called a liar, did not say a word about his incredible experience until 25 years after the war ended. Even then he only wrote about it in his diary, which was recently discovered by Leland W. Thornton, a college history teacher, researcher and author from Centreville. In the March/April 1991 issue of *Michigan History* magazine, Thornton published portions of Downey's diary, which told of the following events.

On a hot, humid August 7, 1864, 18-year-old Downey and his best friend, Daniel Baldwin, lie sweating with the rest of Company E, 11th Michigan Infantry, in shallow trenches near Atlanta, Georgia. Along the edge of a woods a hundred or so yards away was the first of two lines of Confederate entrenchments they would soon attack.

Shortly after 3 p.m. the assault began. Downey's regiment, made up of men from southwest Michigan, marched with the rest of the Union brigade across an open field toward the enemy. Puffs of smoke rose from muskets, and artillery roared as the Union soldiers charged over and past the enemy's first line of trenches, driving the Confederate soldiers back to their second line of defense, deep into the woods. The Union Army then dropped back to the safety of the Confederate ditches they had overrun.

As they dug in during the night, Downey and his comrades counted their losses. Twenty Union soldiers died in the battle, 146 were wounded, and seven were unaccounted for. One of the missing men was Daniel Baldwin.

During the next three days, both armies fortified their positions and fired random shots at each other. But there were no more major attacks, and Downey had plenty of time, especially at night, to agonize over the unknown fate of his friend. Had Baldwin been captured? Was he lying wounded? Or was he dead?

Just before dawn on August 10, Downey's company was ordered back across the field to their original encampment, out of the line of fire. There, the next morning, their welcome hot breakfast was interrupted by a startling sight. Staggering from the battle area was one of the regiment's missing men, George Lockwood.

Lockwood looked like one of the living dead, thought Downey. During the fight a Confederate bullet had torn through the fleshy part of Lockwood's neck. As he screamed in pain, a second shot had entered his open mouth and slammed out the back of his head, instantly knocking him unconscious to the ground. Then a third musket ball had ripped open a foot-long gash down his back.

In spite of the severe wounds and the fact that he had lain untreated in the sweltering heat for three days, somehow Lockwood had survived. But to Downey, the living Lockwood looked more grotesque than the rotting battlefield corpses the teen soldier had seen. Numb after helping the regiment's physician treat Lockwood, Downey was sure he could be shocked no more. He was wrong.

That night Downey awoke from a restless sleep. Looking up, in the light of a full moon he saw another soldier reeling and staggering from the direction of the battlefield. As the man got closer, Downey was stunned to see that it was his friend Daniel Baldwin. He looked as horrible as Lockwood had — sunken eyes, hollow cheeks and ashen face. Downey jumped to his feet and started to shout for help. But Baldwin put his finger to his lips, signaling Downey to be quiet.

Baldwin then turned back toward the battlefield and motioned to Downey to follow him. "He's delirious and disoriented," thought Downey as he ran after Baldwin to bring him back. Downey caught up to his friend at the edge of the Confederate trenches his comrades had captured during the battle. Baldwin stopped, turned, and tried to speak. His lips moved slowly, but no sound came out. It was as though there was no air in his lungs, thought Downey. A second agonizing attempt to talk also failed, so Baldwin again turned and beckoned to Downey to follow.

Before Downey could stop him, Baldwin dropped down into the trench and then climbed up and out the other side. He was headed directly toward the Confederate encampment. "Baldwin, we can't go any farther," Downey whisper-shouted.

But Baldwin didn't stop, and Downey, though exasperated and frightened, followed. A few yards farther, Baldwin veered away from the enemy lines and dropped down to a large patch of thick weeds at the edge of a small creek. He stopped and again turned to face Downey. With his left hand, Baldwin slowly pulled open the breast flap of his uniform coat. In the moonlight Downey could clearly see a large splotch of blood on Baldwin's shirt directly over his heart. With his right hand, Baldwin pointed down into the thick weeds where he stood. Suddenly, Baldwin's human form changed into a shapeless mist and then disappeared.

Confused and terrified, Downey spun around and ran stumbling and falling back to his company for help. He awakened a comrade and breathlessly persuaded the man to go with him back to the spot he had last seen Baldwin. The two men carefully retraced Baldwin's and Downey's route to the stream. After taking a deep breath, they made their way through the tall weeds to the spot Downey had seen Baldwin point to. There lay two dead Union soldiers, their faces too discolored and swollen to be recognizable.

Baldwin and the other man returned to camp, and in the morning a group went out and carried the bodies back on stretchers. Downey watched as the company Captain searched through the dead men's uniform pockets for identification. He pulled back the breast flaps of the coats. On the shirt over one dead man's heart was a huge blood-stain surrounding a hole made by the bullet that killed him. From the coat pocket the Captain pulled a watch inscribed with the name of its owner — Daniel Baldwin.

After the war ended, Downey went on to become a world-renowned professor of mathematics, publishing such works as *Elements of Differentiation and Algebra* and *The New Revelation Through the Spectroscope and the Telescope*. But he was never able to explain the apparition that had led him to his best friend's body.

NORMAN THE FRIENDLY GHOST

One of Fenton's oldest dwellings, often featured on tours of historic homes, is occupied by a harmless but irritating ghost named "Norman," according to several owners. The spirit is named after Reverend Norman Hough, a Baptist minister who died in the house in 1926 at the age of 93.

Not all residents of the otherwise friendly, cheery home have been bothered by Norman. Those who have say that he opens doors, unrolls toilet paper, causes loud crashes like panes of glass shattering, breaks mirrors, plays classical music, creaks around after midnight, and causes other mischief. For instance, one woman who lived in the house hung a kitchen decoration on the wall. As she left the room, she heard it drop to the floor. She returned and secured the piece back on the wall. Before she could turn to leave, the decoration flew off the wall and across the room, knocking an ashtray to the floor and breaking it.

Most of the residents who have been troubled by the clergyman's spirit say they could often temporarily stop the annoyances by yelling something like, "Norman, cut it out!"

THE TORSO OF TAU KAPPA EPSILON

During the late 1970s, residents at an Alma College fraternity claimed their house was haunted by a ghost who made noise and played practical jokes.

Some members of Tau Kappa Epsilon reported catching glimpses of a headless, limbless torso that was covered with a white V-neck T-shirt and floated just above the floor from room to room in the turn-of-the-century house. Others said they turned off mysteriously running showers only to have them go back on as soon as they stepped out of the room.

The ghost was believed to be that of a former member of the fraternity who died in a canoeing accident in 1967.

JUSTICE HAS EYES

A 19-year-old North Branch woman who died after being struck by a hit-and-run driver in 1974 continued to look for her killer through the eyes of her picture, encased in plastic and attached to her tombstone by her parents. According to local legend and several witnesses, the eyes in the picture glowed.

Two years to the day of the accident, a man said to be the one who had caused the young woman's death, drove by the cemetery and, blinded from a sudden intense, shining light from the eyes in the photo, lost control of his car and was killed.

The eyes never glowed again, and the photo was soon removed from the tombstone.

SPIRITS OF PRISONERS PAST

A one-story frame house, built in 1837 in the shadow of the Michigan State Prison at Jackson, plagued the Victor and Beatrice Lincoln family with flying dishes and knives, pounding sounds, and other inexplicable happenings during the early 1960s.

The family had lived in the house for years without any extraordinary happenings. Then late one night in September 1961, Beatrice heard footsteps in the basement, which is located over abandoned tunnels where prisoners had mined coal years earlier. Pounding followed, like someone trying to break a door down. Startled awake by the racket, Victor grabbed a shotgun and went into the basement, but no one was there and the sounds stopped.

Other events followed. Locked doors unlocked and opened. A string of electric Christmas lights suddenly flew from the tree to the floor. Beatrice, while alone in the house, made a bed, left the room, and returned minutes later to find the blankets pulled down. In February 1962 a paring knife flew from the table and struck her in the leg.

A curious probation officer stopped by to investigate, and while he was there, water taps in the bathroom and burners on the gas kitchen stove mysteriously turned on.

Weary and frightened, the Lincolns moved out in 1964. Other families who subsequently lived in the house experienced no problems.

WILL WE HEAR FROM HARRY?

Harry Houdini, the world's best-known escape artist, promised his wife, Beatrice, that if he died before she, he would try to contact her from the afterlife. He even gave "Bess," as he affectionately called her, a secret code so that she would definitely know the message was from him.

When Houdini did leave this earthly stage, it happened unexpectedly in Detroit, Michigan, on October 31, 1926. Relatives, magicians, clairvoyants, mediums, ESP experts and others have tried to contact him ever since. Because Houdini died in Detroit, a large number of seances, rituals and ceremonies have taken place in Michigan. All have ended in failure or, at best, with questionable results. But that hasn't deterred the enthusiasm of several Michiganians who keep trying to find out conclusively if Harry Houdini did discover life after death.

Why is Houdini's spirit one of the most-sought-after ever?

One reason is the vow that Houdini made to his wife. Another is the unique date of his death. Harry Houdini died on Halloween, a time when spirits are said to be free to roam the earth.

But mostly it is the mystical nature of the man himself. Houdini's prime performing years, roughly from 1900 until his death, took place during a time when people's imaginations, not television, replayed what their eyes had seen. Houdini routinely awed audiences by doing the "impossible," such as breaking out of Scotland Yard's best handcuffs, "escape-proof" prisons, sealed coffins, locked vaults and safes, and a cooper's inventory of barrels, boxes and other containers fastened shut. His repertoire also included escaping from a submerged, chained-shut packing crate and from a 4-foot-high milk can filled with water and then locked. As a result, many fans and contemporaries — including Sir Arthur Conan Doyle, creator of Sherlock Holmes — were convinced that Houdini possessed supernatural powers.

Probably the feat most responsible for that belief was the Chinese Water Torture Trick. During its performance Houdini was shackled and then suspended and lowered upside down into a tank of water. A nervous assistant drew a curtain around the container then stood ready with an axe for a rescue, if neccesary. It never was. Though more than enough time would pass for an ordinary person to drown, Houdini, dripping wet and smiling, always stepped from behind the curtain to great applause.

Houdini brought his act to Detroit many times. To promote one of those appearances, in November 1906, he leaped off the Belle Isle Bridge after Detroit police officers had securely shackled him with two pairs of handcuffs. While under the frigid water, Houdini freed himself from the cuffs, popped to the surface and, while onlookers applauded and newspaper reporters furiously scribbled notes, swam to a waiting boat.

Another of Houdini's stage and promotional stunts was to challenge selected people to hit his firm abdomen as hard as they could. Of all the "death-defying" stunts Houdini performed, it was that simple feat of strength that cost him his life. After a performance in Montreal on Friday, October 22, 1926, Houdini was relaxing in his dressing room when a fan approached. The young man, not realizing that Houdini wasn't prepared, slammed his fist into the 52-year-old performer's midsection.

The unexpected blow damaged Houdini's appendix. By the time he arrived in Detroit, a day later, for a performance at the Garrick Theater, his temperature was 104 degrees F. After finishing his act on Sunday night, October 24, 1926, Houdini collapsed and was rushed to Grace Hospital. The next morning doctors removed his ruptured appendix. But peritonitis set in and the showman's condition deteriorated. Finally, at 1:26 p.m. on October 31, 1926, in room 401 of Grace Hospital, Harry Houdini died. In the moments before his passing, he renewed his vow to send a coded after-death message to Bess.

Bess kept a light burning under Harry's picture and each year on the anniversary of her husband's death, took part in a seance. After several tries a medium, Arthur Ford, actually transmitted the promised message. Early in their marriage, Bess and Harry had been stage partners, and the secret words were a cue from their old vaudeville mindreading act.

Bess rejoiced that she had proof Harry lived on in the spirit world. Later, however, she was devastated to learn that her husband had had a mistress, to whom he had made the same promise and given the same code. The mistress, it turns out, had passed the "secret" message along to Ford. Bess turned out the light under Harry's picture in 1936, and in 1943 she died, apparently without ever making contact with him.

Houdini never said he'd communicate with anyone other than Bess, but that hasn't kept a host of people from trying. Traditionally, most attempts have taken place annually on Halloween, and decade anniversaries of Houdini's death seem to increase both the number of tries and their intensity. Members of the media are almost always invited, to verify contact if it happens. Following is a sampling of recent attempts to communicate with Harry from Michigan.

October 31, 1976 — On the 50th anniversary of Houdini's death, a group of magicians gathered at Grace Hospital and performed a wand-breaking ritual, as done at Houdini's funeral. One participant tried to record Houdini's response on videotape but only picked up interference from a local rock station.

October 31, 1978 — On the 52nd anniversary of the death of Houdini, who was 52 when he died, two female mediums, the two men who organized the seance, and six reporters gathered in Grace Hospital's Room 401, which had been converted to a storage room. One medium said she received the message, "Mishigoss," Yiddish for "ridiculous." Some felt that was an appropriate response from Harry Houdini, born Ehrich Weiss, who was Jewish. The other medium said Houdini told her there are three Loch Ness monsters, not just one. This was the last of many seances held in the room where Houdini died. The building was demolished the next year.

October 31, 1978 — At the American Museum of Magic, in Marshall, Michigan, seance participants also appealed to Houdini's Jewish heritage. At 1:26 p.m. they tried to entice Harry by ceremoniously lowering lox and bagels into the milk can from which he used to escape. One of the members, who gathered in a circle around the container, reported feeling a vague "vibration."

May 23, 1989 — The Amazing Kreskin and Bob Lund, curator of the American Museum of Magic, decided the best way to get a message to Harry might be through Bess. So they gathered five other people at the American Museum of Magic and, in the presence of representatives of 10 news organizations, held a seance to try to contact Houdini via his dead widow. A Houdini poster suspended from the ceiling swung gently, and a lock on one of Houdini's containers moved slightly.

So far, Houdini has apparently declined the call for a spiritual encore. But there's little doubt, especially with the 70th and 75th anniversaries of his death approaching, that people will keep trying. Why? As Houdini himself said, "The will to believe is powerful."

UNIDENTIFIED FLYING OBJECTS

People in all parts of the world have seen unidentified flying objects (UFOs) moving through the skies practically since the dawn of recorded history. Stone carvings show that UFOs may have been observed by the Chinese some 45,000 years ago. Around 1500 B.C. an Egyptian pharaoh and his subjects were frightened by mysterious, foul-smelling "circles of fire" that dropped out of the sky one night and then flew away. The *Bible* chronicles a sighting by the prophet Ezekiel, who watched a winged, fiery object fly out of a whirlwind in 532 B.C. Seventeen centuries later a large group of Japanese farmers saw a silvery disc swoop down from the clouds and skim over their fields. Astronomers peering through telescopes in several countries during the 1800s recorded occasional sightings of unusual disc-shaped flying objects. From the turn of the 20th century, when humans themselves finally took to the air, reported UFO sightings have steadily increased to a current level of thousands per year.

A 1990 Gallup survey, in fact, revealed that one in seven Americans say they have personally seen a UFO. People who report sightings come from a cross-section of social, educational and economic backgrounds, but there are a few trends. Not surprisingly, those who "believe in" UFOs see them more than those who don't. People in rural areas see more UFOs than urban dwellers. Young people see more UFOs than old people. And people who are out after dark see the most UFOs. Many reports, in fact, come from law enforcement officers working the night shift.

No matter who sees UFOs or where, the sightings are remarkably consistent. Most people observe mysterious bright, colored lights that move rapidly. Others see actual physical entities, usually unrecognizable disc-, oval-, needle- or cigar-shaped metallic objects that hover, wobble, and maneuver at tremendous speeds.

Almost all of those *un*identified flying objects, however, turn out to be identifiable or at least explainable. Nature, for instance, often plays tricks on people's eyes and minds. Strangely shaped clouds, birds, ball lightning, "earthquake lights," and planets, meteors, and other astronomical bodies are some of the natural phenomena commonly reported as UFOs.

Manmade objects, too, can take on an other-worldly look. Reflections of the sun off the bright surfaces of airplanes, for instance, can give the appearance of discs or other strange metallic shapes moving through the sky. Unusually shaped experimental aircraft account for a few sightings. Other human creations mistakenly reported as UFOs include satellites, missiles, kites, searchlights, aircraft navigation and anticollision beacons, jet engine exhaust, condensation trails, and research and weather balloons. In fact, weather balloons, which reflect light and can move erratically with rapidly fluctuating air currents, account for as many as a fourth of all UFO sightings.

Some UFO reports are fakes or hoaxes. A particularly mysterious UFO that appeared in the sky over Holland, Michigan, one night in 1967, for instance, turned out to be a lit candle suspended under a balloon that was launched by teenagers.

And a few UFO sightings, sadly, are manifestations of overactive imaginations — delusions if you will — often brought on by loneliness or stress.

Most of the lengthy list of possible UFO identifications and explanations was compiled during an extensive U.S. Air Force study of the phenomena. Starting in 1948, civilian scientists and Air Force experts teamed up under the code name Project Blue Book to investigate UFO sightings across the country. Over the next 22 years, researchers checked out more than 12,000 UFO reports and officially determined the cause in 95 percent of the cases.

The remaining 5 percent defied conventional explanation. But given enough time and money, said the Air Force, they were certain they could identify all of the remaining mystery objects or prove that the sightings were not valid. Therefore, they concluded, there was no reason to continue the investigation, and in 1970 Project Blue Book was terminated.

The Air Force's convoluted conclusion did not satisfy many reputable scientists or reassure a good portion of the American public. Most of the 700 or so strange objects still on the "unidentified" list had been seen by rational, intelligent, well-qualified individuals whose integrity could not be doubted. And what they had observed could in no way, even as Project Blue Book itself determined, "be correlated with any known object or phenomena."

The unsolved Project Blue Book cases also left unanswered the often unspoken question at the core of the UFO controversy. Are any UFOs piloted or controlled by intelligent life forms from another part of our galaxy or universe?

It doesn't seem to matter much whether the possibility is real or remote. Just the idea that we might not be alone in our cold, bleak universe has long been the source of curiosity, fascination, fear and even hope. Hundreds of books, each with a unique perspective, have examined the UFO phenomena. H.G. Wells' famous 1938 "War of the Worlds" radio broadcast (still available on audio cassettes) sent the nation into panic. Hollywood films such as *E.T.* and *Close Encounters of the Third Kind* attract huge audiences, and television programs often feature alien-visitor story lines. Front-page headlines of supermarket tabloids regularly announce not only UFO visits, but also landings and occasional abductions of humans. Even the mainstream media — including the staid *New York Times*, newspaper, the news departments at all three major television networks, and *Life, Time,* and *Newsweek* magazines — have dealt seriously with the subject. And dozens of individuals and groups — some scientific, some lay, some off the wall — continue to investigate the origins of UFOs.

A few UFO researchers operate out of Michigan. Since 1989 Western Michigan University's Prof. Michael Swords has served as the editor of *The Journal of UFO Studies,* which deals with very technical subjects such as chemical analyses of substances found at reported landing sites. And John Shepherd (see p. 91) of Bellaire has spent more than a quarter million dollars of his own money in a more than 20-year attempt to contact extraterrestrials.

A Flushing, Michigan, couple currently serve as executives of a private international organization called the Mutual UFO Network (MUFON). George Coyne is MUFON's central regional director for 20 states, and his wife, Shirley, is the group's Michigan director. The Coynes say they have not only seen dozens of UFOs themselves but also that they have been abducted by aliens several times and have carried on conversations with them.

According to the Coynes, UFO incidents in Michigan often number into the hundreds each year, and their claim is generally backed up by a variety of objective sources including law enforcement agencies. It's safe to say, then, that over the past 40-50 years there have been several thousand sightings of UFOs in Michigan skies. Almost all, however, ultimately have been or could be filed under the headings, "unreliable," "unverifiable" or "explainable."

There are, however, a few close encounters of the Michigan kind that have become classics in the casebooks of ufologists.

AN UNBELIEVABLE CASE OF GAS

One of the most remarkable and widely publicized UFO events — *anywhere, ever* — occurred in southeast Michigan in March 1966.

The week-long series of incidents began with what seemed to be just another of the hundreds of "routine," explainable and then forgettable UFO sightings that take place in Michigan each year.

On March 14, at about 4 a.m., two Washtenaw County sheriff's deputies observed an unusual object, marked by red and green lights, moving rapidly — up, down, sideways, often stopping suddenly — in the northwestern sky. The unidentified object was soon joined by a second, similarly lighted object, and the two then appeared to fly in formation. About an hour later, two more UFOs joined the original pair and the four flew off together.

The two amazed deputies weren't the only ones who watched the predawn air show. Sheriff's departments in Washtenaw, Monroe and Livingston counties and police departments in Ypsilanti, Dexter, and Sylvania, Ohio, were flooded with calls from local citizens who saw the strange, bright-colored objects. Personnel at Selfridge Air Force Base, in Mt. Clemens, also said they saw the UFOs but were unable to identify them or pick them up on radar.

Three nights later, several of the objects appeared again at about 4 a.m. but this time in the southern sky. And again, law enforcement officers and residents in Washtenaw, Livingston and Monroe counties watched as the brightly lit UFOs maneuvered at fantastic speeds — hovering, diving, climbing, turning sharply, flying in line formation — for nearly three hours. This time Selfridge Air Force Base confirmed the movements with radar tracking, and a few sheriff's deputies got a closer look through binoculars. The UFOs, they said, appeared to be disc-shaped and glowed in a variety of bright colors ranging from green to red.

Those sightings, though remarkable, were only preliminaries to two main events.

On March 20 at about 8:30 p.m., 47-year-old Frank Mannor and his 19-year-old son, Ron, saw a bright object fall from the sky into a wooded swamp about a half mile from their Dexter-area farm. Thinking it was probably a meteor, they put on rubber hip boots and set out to investigate. After slogging several hundred yards into the marsh, they stopped, stunned. There, hovering just above wisps of ground fog about 500 yards in front of them, was a glowing car-size, football-shaped object whose brown surface was pitted "like coral." Its center pulsed with a red glow, and on each end was a smaller flashing light. Not only did the thing not emit any noise, it seemed to absorb sound to create an absolute, eerie silence.

The Mannors stood transfixed for nearly half an hour as the object hovered, rose and fell erratically. Then the UFO suddenly lurched a few yards toward the Mannors. They turned and ran back to the farm, where they called police.

Given the strange happenings during the previous week, more than a dozen Washtenaw County Sheriff's Department deputies in several patrol cars responded to the Mannors' call. They were quickly followed by 30-40 bystanders attracted by the commotion. By the time the officers and audience arrived, four more lighted UFOs were hovering in a quarter circle just above the treetops where the Mannors had seen the object on the ground. Several deputies moved cautiously on foot into the swamp. But before they could get as close as the Mannors had, the object on the ground took off with a sound described by many of the witnesses "like the echo of a ricocheting bullet."

For the next several minutes, all five UFOs alternately hovered over the treetops, dipped into the swamp, and appeared to land and take off again, all without making a sound. When several of the objects set a course directly over the road, officers in six patrol cars chased them. One UFO then abruptly turned, dipped down to hover briefly only 10 feet over one of the cars, and rose again. The five objects joined in formation and then suddenly vanished from the night sky.

The police interviewed all witnesses and then, coupled with their own observations, put together a composite description of the UFOs. They were roughly triangular in shape and appeared to have a "quilted" surface. Each had a V-shaped antenna protruding from its undercarriage. They weren't identical, however. The UFO that had taken off from the swamp was larger than its four "sister ships." And the flashing lights on each varied in color and intensity from object to object.

The incredible details of the Dexter incident hadn't yet reached the residents at a Hillsdale College women's dormitory when, the next evening, they too saw a large, glowing football-shaped object rise out of a swamp only a few hundred yards away. Eighty-seven students plus several adults, including the college's dean and the county's civil defense director, witnessed what happened next.

For the next four hours, the unknown lighted object alternately hovered and rapidly but erratically maneuvered over the campus. At one point it flew directly at the dormitory, then stopped suddenly and retreated back to the swamp. A few witnesses reported that the object also "dodged around an airport beacon light."

The object glowed with an intense silver light that sometimes rapidly changed to red, said most witnesses. Some reported they also saw smaller individual lights, and a few related that the object's luminosity dimmed when vehicles, especially police cars, approached, then brightened again when the vehicles left. Its dimensions appeared to vary too, from car-size to nearly 20 feet across, though it was hard to tell because it didn't have a definite shape. The civil defense director, however, who watched through binoculars, said that the object was definitely some kind of craft. Whatever it was disappeared back into the swamp from which it came.

Within a few days virtually every newspaper in the country plus national radio and television news shows featured stories about the Dexter/Hillsdale UFOs. The reports generated a tremendous amount of public pressure, especially in Michigan, for an investigation and explanation.

The Air Force responded quickly. Too quickly. A day after the Hillsdale sighting, Dr. J. Allen Hynek, an astrophysicist and UFO expert from Northwestern University who served as a civilian consultant to the Air Force, arrived in Michigan in the company of several Air Force officers. As Hynek organized his investigation, reports of more UFOs flooded in from around the state. Convinced that Michigan residents were living in a state of near mass hysteria, the Air Force high command urged Hynek to immediately offer an explanation. Hynek replied that he had barely begun investigating and had no idea, as yet, what had caused the sightings. The Air Force ordered him to debunk the reports anyway.

So on March 25, only four days after the Hillsdale incident, Hynek called a press conference and told reporters that, because of the marshy locations of both sightings, it was possible that swamp gas may have caused the unusual phenomena. Air Force Major Hector Quintanilla, who was the head of Project Blue Book (see p. 68) at the time, followed by saying he was classifying the Michigan sightings as "explained," and the "experts" left the state.

The token investigation infuriated then House Republican minority leader Gerald R. Ford and other Michigan congressmen, who demanded that the U.S. House of Representatives conduct their own inquiry. On April 5, 1966, The House Armed Services Committee responded by holding the first-ever Congressional hearing on UFOs. But the committee called only three witnesses — Hynek, Quintanilla, and Air Force Secretary Harold Brown — quizzed them in a one-day closed session, and then dropped the matter.

The quick-fix "swamp gas" theory subjected Hynek and the Air Force to worldwide ridicule that has yet to end. "Must be swamp gas" is still a standing joke automatically recited as an explanation for any mysterious phenomenon.

To this day there has been no other explanation or reappearance of the Dexter/Hillsdale UFOs.

SEARCH AND DESTROYED

At about 6 p.m. on November 23, 1953, Air Defense Command radar equipment at Kinross Air Force Base, Sault Ste. Marie, Michigan, locked on an unidentified object flying over Lake Superior. A lone F-89 jet fighter and its two-man crew were sent up to investigate and, if possible, get close enough to observe and identify the unknown aircraft. The interceptor climbed to an altitude of 8,000 feet as it headed northwest in pursuit. Radar observers on the ground watched the blip from the jet close in on and then catch up to the blip from the mystery object, about 60 miles off Keweenaw Point. Suddenly, both radar blips merged, then disappeared from the screen.

With unusual candor and speed, the Air Force Public Information Office immediately released details of the incident and said the sudden disappearance of both blips indicated that a collision had occurred.

Only hours later, however, the Air Force retracted that story and offered a second account of what had happened. Radar operators had misread the scope, the two blips had not merged, and there was no collision said an Air Force spokesman. According to the new version, the American fighter pilot had actually intercepted and identified the unknown craft as an offcourse Royal Canadian Air Force C-47 transport. The F-89 then had turned to head back to base and during the return flight crashed into Lake Superior. Probably, said the Air Force report, the pilot suffered an attack of vertigo and lost control of his plane.

Officials and experts were quick to question the credibility of that account. A representative of the chief of staff of the Royal Canadian Air Force stated that they had no record of any visual, radar or radio contact between one of their C-47s and a USAF F-89 on November 23, 1953. In fact, they added, none of their C-47s had flown anywhere near where the F-89 disappeared. Experienced aviators also attacked the vertigo theory. The officer in command, they said, could have simply switched on the automatic pilot until the vertigo passed, or the copilot could have temporarily taken over the controls.

To accept the U.S. Air Force explanation, said the skeptics, meant believing that skilled radar technicians had no idea what they were doing, that the Royal Canadian Air Force had no idea where their planes were, and that both F-89 pilots had lost control of themselves or their plane.

If the Air Force account was unbelievable, what then *had* happened in the eerie blackness just off the Michigan coast? What had caused the F-89 and its pilots to vanish?. No trace of the airmen or their plane was ever found.

Dozens of UFO researchers have studied the event in the ensuing years and have come up with a couple of scenarios they say fit the facts as originally presented. One is that the F-89 caught up to a UFO and accidentally rammed it, causing a collision in which both aircraft were obliterated. Others think that an alien UFO either destroyed or captured the F-89 then disappeared at a speed beyond the capabilities of radar to monitor, or by instantly translating itself into another state or dimension.

Either way, the ufologists suspect, the U.S. Air Force has covered up a close encounter of the worst kind.

AFTER-HOURS VISITOR

In 1978 Dr. Harry Willnus, a history and government teacher at Romulus High School, received a report of a remarkable UFO sighting in his area. In turn, Willnus — who, at the time, was a volunteer investigator for the Center for UFO Study in Evanston, Illinois — related the following events to a *Detroit News* reporter.

As a ranger prepared to close up the Lower Huron Metropolitan Park in Romulus at 10:45 p.m. on February 8, 1978, he noticed flashing lights in the sky. At first that didn't strike the young man as unusual, since Metropolitan Airport was only a couple of miles away. But as he drove through the park to make sure there weren't any people who might be locked in when he closed the gates, the source of the lights followed him.

Suddenly the object swooped in so close that the surprised young ranger swerved his vehicle into a snowbank to avoid it. When he looked back up through the windshield, the craft was still there, hovering above the treetops about 150 yards away. He couldn't make out what it was, only that it had blue, yellow, green, orange and white lights. And eerily, there was no engine noise or any other sound coming from it. The young ranger radioed his partner, an older man who was patrolling nearby.

When the second ranger arrived, he shined a powerful spotlight onto the mysterious object. Both men stared in awe and disbelief as the light revealed a solid, glossy, gray metallic object shaped like a sombrero. Circling its outer edge were hundreds of tiny white lights, which looked like a row of windows. In the older ranger's previous 20 years in the Air Force, he had come across no aircraft that even remotely looked or moved like this one.

The object silently darted around the treetops for several more minutes, then disappeared.

CURIOUS OR DANGEROUS?

Over a 13-day period in November 1975, a number of UFOs were seen over Strategic Air Command Bases in Michigan, as well as in North Dakota and Montana. According to the book, *Are There Alien Beings?*, some of the objects hovered over nuclear weapons storage areas, and a black tubular-shaped object emerged from the underside of one of the unknown craft. F-106 interceptors were sent up, but the UFOs dimmed their lights and disappeared.

SUPERIOR UFOS

In early August 1966, according to a United Press International (UPI) report, enlisted men at a U.S. Air Force radar base on the Keweenaw Peninsula reported "solid radar contact" with seven to 10 unidentified flying objects moving at about 9,000 mph in a "V" formation over Lake Superior. Two other radar stations, one in Minnesota and one in North Dakota, also spotted the objects, and a third station, in Canada, reported electronic jamming of its radar.

Jet interceptors gave chase over Duluth, Minnesota, but could not maintain the speed of the UFOs and were easily outdistanced.

BIGFOOT SIGHTINGS

For the past several hundred years, a rare and mysterious life form has moved through the minds and lives of people — often entire societies — around the globe. No matter who has talked of the creature, and no matter when and where the stories are told, the descriptions are similar — a 7- to 8-foot-tall, 500- to 700-pound hairy giant that resembles an ape but walks erect like a human.

In Nepal the creature is known as the Yeti or Abominable Snowman. Aboriginal Australians call it Yowie. In Russia it's the Alma. In Canada and the U.S. Pacific Northwest it goes by the name Sasquatch. Throughout the rest of the United States, it's been dubbed Bigfoot because of the 17- to 20-inch-long footprints people say it has left in snow, mud or dirt.

Tracks, in fact, most often are the only evidence offered of Bigfoot's existence. No one has ever captured or killed one of the man-beasts. The few photos or film offered up as proof have been, at best, inconclusive; at worst, staged. "Reliable" sightings of the shy, elusive creature, which is said to inhabit only the world's remotest areas, are rare. One source, for instance, says that there have been only about a thousand bona fide glimpses of Bigfoot in North America during the past 200 years.

Some have occurred in Michigan. Michigan Indians, in fact, may have first sighted Bigfoot three or four centuries ago says Wayne King, a Bigfoot expert from Caro. King, who is director of the Michigan/Canadian Bigfoot Information Center (see p. 94), says that a Michigan species of Bigfoot exists and that there are probably several hundred of them roaming through untouched areas of Michigan wilderness.

Is there such a creature as Bigfoot? If so, does it make a home in Michigan's vast forest lands? Most reputable scientists dismiss both thoughts as fantasy. The experts, however, would have a hard time convincing some very sane, normal, rational Michigan residents and visitors who have had some very unusual experiences. To them, Bigfoot is a very real possibility.

TRACKS AROUND BARRYTON

Becky Kurtz opened her back door the morning of September 3, 1977, to a puzzling sight. Her family's two normally fearless German shepherd/huskie-mix watchdogs were wimpering and cowering on the cement stoop. When she opened the door, the terrified dogs shot inside to the basement, where they hid for two days.

Though Becky and her husband, Bob, had moved into their small, rural Barryton home only a week before, the dogs had adjusted well. Normally, they lay outside the back door peering some 300 yards across a plowed field to the Hughs Swamp, which sprawls 14 miles to connect with the even more-vast Martiny Lake flowage.

The Kurtz's dogs weren't the only animals to behave strangely. Numerous whitetail deer that usually came out each day at dawn and dusk to feed on apples in a small, grassy orchard close to the house also disappeared.

Several days later Bob brought some trash to a metal burning barrel at the rear of their property. There, he noticed some huge indentations in the bare soil. They were like no animal tracks he had ever seen. The prints measured 16½ inches long and 9½ inches wide, and the distance between them — the stride of whatever left them — was nearly 5 feet.

Kurz followed the tracks for 60-70 feet to where they disappeared into the orchard. Along the way milkweeds and other plants had been crushed where each foot had come down. Most tracks were imbedded 1½ to 2 inches deep into the ground.

Curious, Kurtz removed his shoes and socks and walked barefoot in the soil near some of the tracks. The 180-pound man's size-10½ foot sank in only a half inch.

Kurtz called in two other area residents, Gene Little and George McClain, for their opinion. Little was a long-time wildlife photographer and producer who had often shot film for the "Michigan Outdoors" television program. McClain was an experienced big-game hunter. It didn't take them long to agree that whatever had left the footprints weighed close to 800 pounds.

Both also agreed it couldn't have been a bear. When Little and McLain examined the ground closely, they found no telltale round prints that would have been made by a bear's front paw. And if a huge bear somehow, for some reason, had managed to walk on its hind legs over such a long distance, it could never have managed a stride of five or six feet, they said. Also, a bear moving in an upright position would have a straddle-legged gait. The tracks on the Kurtz property ran in a straight, human-like pattern. Little shot footage of the tracks for a Grand Rapids television station, and Kurtz made plaster casts of them. One exceptionally clear casting showed a huge five-toed foot with no claws.

Little, who died within the year, said on a taped account, "I don't see how it can be a hoax. The prints showed an ape-like toed foot with a definite ball imprint, not the kind of forgeries that would be left by someone wearing 'fake feet.' " If someone instead had pounded a hand-crafted, molded foot into the relatively hard soil, the resulting tracks would have been shallow and uniform. The prints behind the Kurtz home were deep and varied — all in all, very "natural looking." And, as Little and McLain observed, there were no tracks in the easiest place for a prankster to have placed them, the adjacent, freshly plowed field.

Little came to a conclusion shared by McClain, the Kurtzes, and anyone else who has investigated the origin of the tracks — "There is no good, logical answer."

UNWANTED HOUSE GUEST

In 1977 Zane Gray, a retired State Police lieutenant, paid what he expected to be a routine, early morning visit to a remote gorge near Lake Ann where he was building a house. He arrived, however, to find 27 unusual, huge tracks imbedded in the soft soil. The 18-inch-long prints, which showed a flexible ape-like toed foot with a ball imprint, had been sunk deep into the dirt by something with great weight. Less than a week later, Gray found more such tracks on a nearby road.

Gray, who later became sheriff of Benzie County, now says, "At the time I was open to the possibility of a Bigfoot. There had been sightings in the area and mysterious noises. But now that all this time has elapsed without finding one, I think somebody probably made the tracks. But yet, I have absolutely no idea how."

SIGHTINGS AT BATTLE CREEK

In 1981 the *Battle Creek Enquirer* reported several sightings of a "9-foot hairy creature" in and around the Fort Custer State Recreation Area.

In one incident, according to the paper, Bill Kosmider, a recreation supervisor, and state trooper Paul Uerling, from the Hastings Post, "saw a huge creature on the frozen surface of a beaver pond" while they were making the rounds of adjacent military land in a park truck one evening. By the time the pair moved in for a closer look, however, the thing had disappeared.

BIGFOOT HUNTER COMES CLOSE

Wayne King, Director of the Michigan/Canadian Bigfoot Information Center (see p. 94), says he personally has seen Bigfoot on three separate occasions. Two of the sightings were brief glimpses.

The third, his closest encounter, took place in 1978. King received a call on his Bigfoot-sighting hotline and drove the short distance from his home in Caro to a rural area near Kingston. There in the twilight, King said he got a good look at not one, but two of the creatures on the forest's edge. One was much smaller than the other, possibly an offspring thought King.

King had left his home office in such a hurry, he had forgotten to strap on the holstered .357-magnum pistol he always carries on his Bigfoot investigations. So, King said, he called the State Police for help.

Just as a patrol car approached, the creatures slipped into the forest. King and a trooper went into the woods after them and got close, but couldn't see anything because of the darkness.

"It was the only time I have known fear," King was reported as saying. "We could hear them breathing. I knew we were gonna be hit. I could feel it coming. I heard the trooper take the safety off his gun. And then there was silence."

CROSSING BIGFOOT

During the summer of 1979, Nicholas Zurawic and his fiancee, Abby Matthews, were driving on US-27 toward what was supposed to be a routine, relaxing up-north weekend. About 50 miles north of Midland, the couple, both senior law students at the University of Michigan, saw three huge, hairy creatures dash across the road ahead of them.

"At first I thought they were people, but they were moving as fast as deer," Zurawic said in a taped account of the incident. "I just couldn't believe what I was seeing. They weren't human."

An investigation revealed that a fence off the highway at the spot had been broken through.

BUCKEYES BATTLE BIGFOOT

During a 1976 training session, two Ohio National Guardsmen were assigned to spend the night in a personnel carrier in an isolated area of their camp near Grayling. In the pre-dawn hours, the men were awakened by something pounding on the vehicle. They clicked on their flashlights. Spotlighted in the beams was a huge, hairy ape-like animal. The lights evidently angered the creature, said the

guardsmen, because it made menacing growling sounds and continued pounding as it climbed on top of the vehicle.

The men radioed for help, and military policemen who arrived at
the scene spotted the creature disappearing into the woods by a
nearby lake.

An investigation revealed that the incident was not a prank and
that the two men had not been drinking.

SEEKERS OF THE
UNKNOWN

Most people are reluctant to admit that they "believe in" or even give much thought to UFOs, Bigfoot, ghosts, and psychics, ESP, and other paranormal happenings.

There are, however, a few singular Michigan residents who not only believe in those and other phenomena but also actively and seriously investigate them. Each has become an expert in a field he knows most people consider to be frivolous or unbelievable. All have dedicated the better part of their adult lives plus, in some cases, small fortunes to pursuits they know are, in the words of John Lennon, like "trying to shovel smoke with a pitchfork in the wind."

MICHIGAN'S MOST HAUNTED

There are no such things as ghosts, say skeptics, and the only reason some people believe there are is to deny their own mortality. The skeptics are twice wrong, says Dr. Richard Brooks, chairman of Oakland University's philosophy department. Professor Brooks is convinced that ghosts *do* exist and precisely *because* every one of us does survive death.

Brooks, 55, has not come to that provocative conclusion quickly or frivolously. His interest in paranormal phenomena began more than 40 years ago during his boyhood in the Milwaukee, Wisconsin, area. Years later, as a student majoring in philosophy at Beloit College, the University of Wisconsin and the University of Minnesota, Brooks began to contemplate what might result if the study of philosophy included, or at least didn't outright reject, parapsychology.

When he joined the teaching staff at Oakland University in 1965, he turned thought into action. He started by trying to organize a series of student discussions in parapsychology, but he ran into resistance, even ridicule from his colleagues. "I suddenly realized," he says, "that not only did they not believe in anything paranormal, but their disbelief was based upon no investigation whatsoever. I decided to do something about it."

Brooks spent the next several years contacting parapsychological researchers around the world, visiting their laboratories, and studying the results of their research. As he met and became acquainted with more and more experts, he gained a reputation in Michigan as one of the few academics who was seriously interested in unexplained happenings. Radio stations, newspapers and TV stations often interviewed him or referred to his unique expertise. As a result, listeners, readers and viewers began calling Brooks to tell him about their strange experiences and to ask for help.

Most calls were from people who said, in short, "I think I have a ghost in my house." Brooks often went out to investigate, and over the years Michigan's haunted houses became his paranormal specialty.

After nearly 30 years of study and research, Brooks has concluded that there is definite evidence for what he calls "survival phenomena." "I am convinced that there is some element or dimension of all human beings that is non-physical," he says. "Whatever you call it — soul, psyche, psychic residue or something else — this entity survives the death of the physical body." And these survival entities, according to Brooks, often interact with the physical world.

In other words there are ghosts, and they sometimes make their presence known. And it's not always in creaky century-old farm-houses where someone has died, says Brooks. He has visited near-new suburban homes where a ghost, it seems, has decided it likes the neighborhood and moves in. Nor do ghosts always bother every owner of every haunted house. It's not uncommon, he says, for someone to move into a house and encounter a ghost, move out, and the new owners experience nothing spirited for 20 years. Then when somebody else moves in, the ghost seems to start up again.

The problems caused by most ghosts are usually annoying but harmless, says Brooks. Moving objects, doors that won't open even if they're not locked, a feeling of inner coldness, faucets or lights turned on or off, and phantom footsteps and other strange noises are common symptoms of a haunting.

Some spirits are even benevolent. A ghost in a rural Dryden home that Brooks visited would often cover a small child with an extra blanket during cold nights. And in a Hudson house, an evidently departed homemaker occasionally helped the living housewife by taking baked pies out of the oven.

"The thing that really bothers me," says Brooks, "is how the hell do they do it? If you don't have a physical body, how do you open a door or turn on a faucet? It doesn't make sense, and I don't blame my colleagues at all for being very skeptical. I am puzzled and bewildered by it."

Also puzzling to Brooks is how and why, in some rare circum-stances, survival entities become visible. According to his research, not all living people are capable of seeing the apparitions. "We know that the people who are physically present play a role in the phenom-ena," he says, "but we don't know how. If you see an apparition, somehow you are contributing to it. It's an inter-relationship. We don't know why, but some people are more receptive to them than others."

When ghosts do make an appearance, they often look and act just like normal human beings, he says. "They avoid furniture, they open doors, they do all the things a human being does except they suddenly disappear. At that point you know you're dealing with something unusual."

And dealing with something that unusual can be more than a little disconcerting, which is why many people who think they're being bothered by a ghost seek Brooks' help. He doesn't have a ghostbusters hotline, but he averages dozens of calls a year at his Oakland University office. "I don't go out looking for haunted houses," he says. "I wait until my telephone rings. After people have talked to their priest, doctor, police or whomever and don't get any help and they think they're going crazy, they often contact their nearest university, usually the psychology department. And more often then not they're told, 'Oh, you need to call Brooks over at Oakland University.' "

Brooks' investigations begin as soon as he answers the phone. He listens carefully to callers' stories to see if they "make sense," that is fit in with his own previous investigations and the more than 100 years of research conducted by others. There are patterns and regularities to hauntings, says Brooks, and if he gets reports that are very deviant he begins to suspect that they're made up or that maybe the people involved need psychiatric help. "And I have had people eventually admit to me that they are undergoing psychiatric treatment," he says.

Sometimes Brooks is able to hand out earthly explanations for what people think may be unearthly phenomena. Wind, water pipes, lightning, settling or structural deficiences in a house, windows vibrating with passing traffic, fog, unusual shadows, and animals — especially mice or rats —are just a few causes of ghost-like sights and sounds.

What's left are cases where apparently sane, rational, reasonable people are genuinely concerned that something unexplainably strange is going on. An average of once a year, Brooks and sometimes his students head out into the field to check them out.

Brooks is the first to admit, however, that he is less than thorough and intensive. "Because of my enormous responsibilities at the university, these investigations have to be somewhat superficial," he says. He has never stayed overnight in a haunted house, and he rarely pays more than one visit. And unlike some serious ghost investigators, he doesn't carry equipment like felt overshoes, heat sensors, cameras loaded with infared film, and video and audio recorders.

Rather, he goes to gather anecdotal data and, more importantly, to help people either get rid of unwanted spirits or at least cope with them. The first thing he does is offer reassurance that ghosts are not harmful and therefore need not be frightening. Ghosts, he explains, are essentially ordinary human beings without their bodies. They therefore act in ways that are appropriate to the person who is deceased. And that doesn't usually include danger-producing behavior. "I have never yet run across a case where anyone was hurt by a ghost," says Brooks.

Still, most people feel a lot more comfortable without a ghost around, and so Brooks tells them how to get rid of unwanted spirits. Sometimes it's quite easy, he says. Often a simple shout, "Go away," will do it. According to Brooks, one elderly woman who was bothered nightly by the apparition of her deceased husband finally shouted in exasperation, "Billy, you're dead. You don't belong here anymore." The ghost never reappeared. Acting on Brooks' advice, another woman, who sensed someone behind her every time she washed dishes, held out a towel and asked the spirit to help dry. It never returned. Sometimes ghosts disappear on their own. "It's almost as though somebody is just passing through on their way to some other kind of existence," says Brooks.

But usually, he says, once you have a ghost it's probably there to stay. Either you learn to live with it, or you move on.

FOR ALIEN EARS ONLY

Forty-year-old John Shepherd has spent all of his extra money and every available hour of his adult life in an ongoing attempt to contact beings in outer space. For eight hours every day, he uses $300,000 worth of electronic and computer equipment to broadcast messages he hopes will be picked up by intelligent extraterrestrial life. That makes John Shepherd unique. What makes him truly *remarkable* is that he doesn't care if he ever receives a reply.

Shepherd admits he has always been "different." He says, for instance, that he was once thrown out of school because he "didn't fit in." That was in kindergarten. Born in Grand Rapids, Shepherd moved to the east side of Detroit to live with his grandparents when his family split up following a divorce. Later he moved with his grandparents to a small cedar-sided cottage on the shores of Intermediate Lake near Bellaire. Shepherd quit school at the age of 16 but earned a high-school education at home, largely through correspondence courses.

He displayed an early interest in electrical gadgets and was doing some serious experimenting — "blowing holes in the carpet," as he says — by the age of 12. Science-fiction publications and television shows, especially "Outer Limits," caused Shepherd to also grow increasingly fascinated with the possibility that we may not be alone in the universe. He became convinced that there is life beyond earth when, as a teen-ager he witnessed what he believes was a UFO moving slowly through the night sky over Detroit.

In 1972, at age 20, he decided to dedicate his electronics talents to a serious search for extraterrestrial life. He launched a project he calls STRAT — Special Telemetry Research and Tracking. He began accumulating and using an extraordinary collection of sophisticated electronic apparatus, including computers, to send music and messages to anyone or anything able to listen in outer space.

When Shepherd turned to outer space, he abandoned worldly interests including, as he points out, "women and booze." He also has never held what most people would describe as a "regular" job. He has worked part-time as a gardener, ski-lift operator, and contract laborer for a TV repairman. He sent some of his earnings to Wall Street, and much of his income now comes from stock-market investments he tracks on a computer. He also rents sound equipment to rock groups and rebuilds and repairs video games, televisions, and other electronics equipment.

For 20 years he has used every surplus dollar to increase the power and sophistication of his one-of-a-kind radio station. The small cabin his grandparents left to him upon their death is packed with banks of transmitters, wavering meters, oscilloscopes, voltmeters, potentiometers and buzzing transformers. Much of the equipment was salvaged from old radio stations and power companies across the country. Computer terminals and monitors fill the foyer. In the living room, where Shepherd usually sleeps, are tape recorders and CD players, and hanging overhead are meters, service boards and modules. Controlling and connecting the system are hundreds of switches, patch cords, and thick bundles of cables that snake everywhere.

Several years ago Shepherd tore out the ground floor of half the cottage in order to build four high-voltage accelerators, which now rise from the basement 16 feet to the ceiling. Two relatively inconspicuous radio towers with blinking red lights poke up from between . the spruces on his front lawn.

Shepherd's station totals 50,000 volts of transmitting power capable of broadcasting $1/2$ to $1^1/2$ million miles beyond the earth's ionosphere. Because the signal he uses is ultra-low frequency and is broadcast upward, even residents in nearby Bellaire and Central Lake can't tune in.

To catch the attention of his potential off-earth audience, Shepherd broadcasts music for eight hours each day. His album-oriented format includes New Age, classical, jazz, reggae, rock and African tribal rhythms — anything he feels might emanate a "varying flowing pattern of energy that comes naturally to the intellect of any living thing that can feel." Twenty-four hours a day he also transmits a 16-note arrangement of tones that he says are "mathematically interesting." Alien audiences don't have to put up with any commercials, but Shepherd does regularly interrupt his broadcasts with a station identification as required by the Federal Communications Commission.

And just in case any off-world listeners want to call in, Shepherd is ready. A sophisticated system of scanners, which probe the skies 24 hours a day, is connected to receivers that will sound an alarm should a UFO respond to a Project STRAT broadcast.

That's not likely. First, in cosmic terms Project STRAT's signal doesn't go very far, only about five times farther than the distance of the moon from Earth. The chance of a spacecraft from another galaxy or even solar system taking a speed-of-light Sunday drive near earth and tuning in to Shepherd's broadcasts is probably infinitesimal.

And if an alien ship does happen to come that close, even Shepherd says its crew probably would not attempt contact. "It could be very important for them not to disturb us," he says. "If extraterrestrial intelligences were going to observe a society, they'd likely want to get as close as they could without upsetting or distorting it in order to get accurate observations."

Not only does Shepherd not expect a response, he doesn't much care. To him the Project STRAT process is much more important than the goal. In other words, all the fun is in the doing. "I feel that I've done more than just build a bunch of machines to contact extraterrestrials," he says. "It's like an artist who has an incredibly burning desire to sculpt his one work to its finest degree. My life is filled with a meaning and purpose that many others lack. Even if my search seems futile, I think there's validity in pursuing my dream."

So for four hours every night and every morning, seven days a week, Shepherd places himself amidst his banks of flashing lights and humming instruments and becomes disc jockey to the universe. To an intelligent and appreciative extra-terrestrial audience somewhere, he hopes his program rates #1.

TRACKING BIGFOOT

Does the huge human-looking, yet-apelike creature variously called Abominable Snowman, Yeti, Sasquatch and Bigfoot really exist? And if so, are any of the hairy giants roaming Michigan forests? Anthropologists, zoologists and mythologists say "no" to both. The experts, however, are wrong, say a few dedicated individuals who regularly prowl the wilds of the world in an effort to prove it.

Two of America's best-known Bigfoot investigators operate out of Michigan only 10 miles from one another. Both Wayne King, 56, of Caro and Art Kapa, 60, of Mayville believe that not only does Bigfoot live, but lives in Michigan. And both are deadly serious in their ongoing efforts to independently and conclusively prove it.

King and Kapa both began their unusual quest during the late-1960s, though they didn't know each other then. And both were inspired by the same events. On several mornings during the summer of 1965, workers at a remote northern California road construction site arrived at the job to find 20-inch-long human-like footprints deeply marking the soft dirt. On one occasion something with superhuman strength had apparently hurled full 250-gallon oil drums over a cliff and another time had overturned a flatbed trailer loaded with culverts. Because of the huge size of the tracks left by the unknown, evidently non-human vandal, it was tagged with a name that stuck — "Bigfoot."

During the following months and years, other evidence and sightings of Bigfoot throughout the Pacific Northwest received national coverage. Most famous was a home movie of what appeared to be an 8-foot-tall human/ape-looking creature striding across a field near Del Norde, California. The incidents sparked an interest in King and Kapa that grew to a passion bordering on obsession.

For about 10 years, King and Kapa indulged their interest in Bigfoot separately and on a part-time basis. King had a full-time job at a Flint General Motors plant and Kapa was in the construction business.

Then in 1977 King got serious. He opened what he called the Michigan/Canadian Bigfoot Information Center and named himself director. He installed four business telephones in the fieldstone basement of his Caro home and recruited several volunteer "field investigators." One was Art Kapa.

For three years the two men worked closely together, allies in pursuit of their elusive quarry. When not responding to calls on King's Bigfoot-sighting hotlines, the pair often set out into the Michigan wilderness on weekends and tried to get Bigfoot to come to them. During all-night vigils while sitting on lawn chairs and throwing sardines as bait into the surrounding blackness, King and Kapa spent countless hours talking about what they would do if Bigfoot showed up.

The discussions turned to bickering and then loud arguments. Finally, in 1980 Art Kapa left King and opened his own clearinghouse for sightings, the Bigfoot Investigation Center, in his farmhouse outside Mayville.

On the surface it would seem that the two men are duplicating efforts. File cabinets in both cluttered home offices are stuffed with written "eyewitness accounts," taped depositions and other reports. Walls are covered with newspaper articles about Bigfoot sightings, and shelves hold huge plaster footprints personally cast by both men. Some 25 flagged pins that poke out from a state map above Kapa's desk mark the location of Michigan Bigfoot sightings or evidence. Wayne King prominently displays a football-size lump of feces he says was dropped by a Bigfoot. Both stock an assortment of equipment unique to their venture, such as powerful night lights, auditory sensors, high-tech recording systems, movie and photographic equipment, plaster of Paris, jugs of water, backpacks and sleeping bags. And both agree that several nomadic Bigfoot roam through areas of Michigan wilderness that are seldom if ever visited by man.

Beyond that, nearly everything they say and do is at odds.

Wayne King believes that the Michigan version of Bigfoot is a primitive species of American ape that weighs 500-700 lbs., stands 7-8 feet tall, and is covered with long, gray or black hair. Though the creature walks upright, King emphasizes that it is a lower form of life — a cunning, powerful animal. Art Kapa, on the other hand, says that every Bigfoot, including those in Michigan, is a sensitive creature with human characteristics.

King is on a search and destroy mission. Armed with a .357-Magnum pistol and high-powered rifle, he says he will shoot to kill when he sees Bigfoot so that he can collect a six-figure reward a group in Dallas has offered him for a Bigfoot corpse. He even has an extra-long freezer reserved at a rental company to preserve Bigfoot's body while moving it.

Art Kapa says that since Michigan Bigfoot is part human, it would be immoral, maybe even criminal, to kill it. All he plans to shoot is photographs and videotape.

King enlists the help of "field investigators" he trains to join in the hunt and the kill. Kapa works alone.

King has tried to call Bigfoot with secret chants he says he learned from Salish Indians. Art Kapa says all King's shouts would do is scare off the shy, nervous creatures.

King claims that he, in fact, *has* spotted Bigfoot in Michigan on three separate occasions (see p. 82), although none of the contacts resulted from his attempts at communication. But King says there haven't been any "reliable" sightings or evidence of Bigfoot in Michigan since about 1983, and so he doesn't leave his home office much any more. And his center's phone numbers are now unlisted because, King says, he only wants calls from serious, knowledgable Bigfoot hunters, who already know how to reach him.

On the other hand, when Art Kapa's listed (517-843-6302) Bigfoot hotline rings with a sighting report, he throws his camera equipment into his full-size van and heads out to investigate, usually within minutes. Kapa, however, has never personally seen a Bigfoot and says the last time he saw signs of the creature in Michigan was in 1989 in Hillsdale County. Still, he keeps trying. The retiree tries to spend two weeks each month walking through Michigan forests looking look for signs of Bigfoot on his own.

"We have some tremendously large areas of untouched wilderness in Michigan," Kapa says. "Who knows, who can really say for sure what's living out there?"

"I know Bigfoot creatures are out there," says Wayne King, "and it will be one of history's biggest scientific finds when I kill one. I'm the predator; Bigfoot is my prey."

THE MICHIGAN METAPHYSICAL SOCIETY

Most American soldiers who survived World War II returned home to resume a normal life. When Sol Lewis came back, he pursued a paranormal life.

He didn't plan it that way. In January 1945, not long after he had arrived in France, Lewis was captured and placed in a prisoner of war camp on a mountainside in Germany. It was, he now laughs, "a hell of a place for a Jewish kid from Detroit to be."

After convincing his captors that he was Italian, not Jewish, his thoughts turned to home. He knew that his mother (his father had died 16 years before) would be devastated by the generic "missing in action telegram" she no doubt had received. He desperately wished he could communicate to her that he was alive.

It didn't seem unusual to Lewis, then, that for three nights in a row he had the same dream. He stood before his mother, held out his arms and said, "See, I'm o.k. I'm detained, but I'm o.k. and I'll be back." Lewis forgot about the unusually vivid dreams until he returned home.

But he could not forget what happened in early April 1945. As he tells it . . .

"I was sitting on a knoll overlooking the POW camp and I closed my eyes. Instantly, I'm at a Passover dinner. My father's there with

97

his skull cap and prayer shawl on, and the rest of my family is there, and all the great food is there. I was so ecstatic.

"And suddenly a voice booms into my head, 'Solomon, what is it you would like to know?'

"And without even thinking I said, 'Why does God allow bodies to be burned at Dachau. Why does God allow so many deaths?'

"And the voice said, 'Solomon, there is no death. You take your body off as you do an overcoat. God doesn't give you just 50, 60 or 70 years of life and that's the end. You come back and take a body again. You, Solomon, have already had hundreds of lives.'

" 'And by the way,' added the voice, 'you're going to be liberated a week from today. And you're going to get off the boat in New York on April 28. You have a destiny, Solomon.'

"And, poof, the voice was gone."

"I didn't know what the hell was going on," says Lewis, "but I did know it was unbelievable, and so I wasn't about to tell anyone else about what had happened." That night when a fellow POW who slept next to him came close to "cracking up," however, Lewis related the unusual experience to him. While not really believing it himself, Lewis assured the frightened young soldier to hang on, because they would be free in a week.

One week to the day later, Lewis and his fellow prisoners heard the distant rumble of tanks. They were American, and a few hours later, Lewis and the rest of the camp were liberated. Lewis began to wonder if his vision had been something more than a dream or hallucination.

Lewis, who was severely malnourished, was placed in the sick bay of a ship that was part of a large convoy headed from France to America. Only a day out of port, a colonel who was paying a courtesy visit mentioned to Lewis that the officers aboard all of the ships had started a money pool, a wager, on when they would reach America. Lewis said he *knew* the exact date and told the officer why.

The officer said, "What the hell, it's as good a date for as good a reason as any, and if you're right, Lewis, I'll split the winnings with you." On April 28, as Lewis walked down the gangplank at New York City, the officer tucked an envelope stuffed with money into Lewis' breast pocket. Lewis was now convinced his vision was real, but there was even more to come.

Lewis traveled back to Detroit by train and reunited with his family — his mother, three older sisters and an older brother. While Lewis was overseas, his mother had moved into a new apartment, one he had never seen. Yet, according to Lewis, when he walked through the door, he blurted, "Ma, I've been here."

And she said, "Yes, I know. Three times. And each time you came to me and you held out your arms and said, 'See, I'm all right. I'm detained but I'll be home.' "

Lewis was stunned. "I'd had experiences that I couldn't explain," he says, "and I wanted more than anything else to find out what it was all about." Lewis set out to do exactly that, and the first thing he learned was that his experiences fell into the realm of what is called either or both "metaphysics" (beyond the physical) or "paranormal" (not scientifically explainable).

Lewis was hooked. "I wanted to know more. My foot was on a path." He read every book he could find on the subjects. He regularly attended an annual retreat for metaphysicists in the mountains of Pennsylvania. And he traveled to India and spent a month studying "the untapped powers of the mind" with a renowned guru. After a few years, his wife joined him in what he says is an ongoing pursuit of "knowledge and self-awareness."

During the late 1960s, Lewis, his wife, and another married couple decided to link up with others in the greater Detroit area who shared their mind quest. They informally formed an organization they called the Michigan Metaphysical Society and initially held meetings in the basement of Lewis' home. But as membership grew over the next 25 years, the society expanded into a complex of rented buildings on 12 Mile Road in Berkley that now includes offices, a 100-seat auditorium, and a bookstore.

The purpose of the society is to expand awareness of almost all unexplained or unexplainable phenomena. That covers a lot of territory, a fact that quickly becomes obvious while browsing the shelves of the society's bookstore. A small sampling from the wide-ranging selection of reference, motivational, and how-to titles includes books on

Channeling — The process of communicating information from non-physical entities through a human being known as a "channel." Channels are also sometimes called "mediums." The channel usually enters into an altered state of consciousness and then takes on the voice and mannerisms of whatever non-worldly entity happens to be communicating — variously angels, nature spirits, totems, guardian spirits, the Higher Self, deities, demons, extraterrestrials, or spirits of the dead.

Clairvoyance — The power to perceive objects, events or people that are out of the natural range of human senses.

Out-of-Body Experiences — A phenomenon, also called "astral projection," in which a person feels separated from his or her physical body and seems to be able to travel to and perceive distant locations on Earth or even in non-wordly realms. Sol Lewis says his wartime visit to his mother's apartment, for example, was most likely an out-of-body experience.

Past-life Recall — The belief that we all have a non-physical essence that returns repeatedly in new physical bodies (reincarnation) and that we can, under certain conditions, remember some of our past lives.

Psychic Power — The ability to acquire or perceive past, present or future information without using any of the five "normal" senses—sight, hearing, smell, touch or taste.

Psychokinesis — The ability to move objects, bend metal, or otherwise influence matter by using only mind power.

Telepathy — Communication through means other than the normal physical senses.

Guest lecturers from around the world plus long-time society members also conduct regularly scheduled lectures, discussion groups, and workshops that cover the metaphysical spectrum.

Because they delve into areas where few minds dare or care to go, society members have been variously characterized as everything from a "collection of gullibles" to "disciples of the devil." One thing they're rarely accused of, however, is being impartial or objective. Though one of the expressed goals of the society is to "investigate paranormal phenomena," members don't set out to scientifically analyze, explain, prove or disprove unusual happenings.

The society's philosophy is that the mind of every "ordinary" human being has extraordinary, even phenomenal capabilities. Therefore, "investigate" to them seems to mean "accept and encourage." If you say you are psychic, to the society you are. If you say you've had an out-of-body experience, to the society you have. If you say you can remember some of your past lives, to the society you do.

"We don't put anything down as a possibility," says Lewis, a practicing hypnotherapist who has taught college courses in parapsychology. "People can and do experience phenomena. It may be unexplainable, but it is their reality."

And he adds that it's not *what* happens that counts anyway. "Paranormal phenomena has its place," he says. "But phenomena isn't the medium, it's the message. The medium is the mind. All we want to do is provoke people's thinking."

UNSOLVED MURDERS

Most people are surprised to learn that, on average, 900 murders are committed in Michigan each year. But even more shocking is the fact that, in a typical year, more than a third of those killings go unsolved.

Authorities give several reasons for that disturbing statistic. Sometimes investigators know before the body is cold that they're not likely to find the murderer. Professional killers who perform "contract hits," for instance, are both experienced and adept at avoiding identification. And in an ever-increasing number of frustrating and frightening cases, victims have been killed purely at random, for no apparent reason.

The rising rate of lawlessness in general also contributes to the number of unsolved slayings. Robberies, muggings and any other crimes where murder is a byproduct, resulting either intentionally or unintentionally, are very difficult to solve, say police. "You usually start with about a million suspects, no witnesses, and a minimal amount of evidence," says one experienced officer.

But the main reason for the high rate of unsolved murders, say most homicide investigators, is that they don't get help and support from the public like they used to. For whatever reasons more and more people — even witnesses — are reluctant or refuse to get involved, to talk to law enforcement officers. All too often it seems that nobody cares except the police and the victims' families.

And though they may want to, the police usually aren't able to care for long. Officially a homicide case remains open until someone is convicted. But realistically, if no good leads or suspects turn up after a few months of investigation, unsolved case files are set aside while more recent murders take priority.

Likewise, unsolved murders usually fade quickly from the public's concern or interest. Headlines move to back page stories to cold statistics in a matter of weeks. That's because, while almost all slayings are sad and tragic, there's usually nothing else particularly remarkable or memorable about them.

The shock waves from a few unsolved murders, however, radiate well beyond their time and place. Some killings appeal to our tabloid instincts because they involve prominent or famous people. Or the sensational circumstances that surround some unsolved murders fascinate us. Other cases nag at us, especially when it seems as though someone very cunning, deliberate and cold may have committed the perfect crime. And finally, it's difficult to forget some unsolved murders because they unexpectedly and violently end otherwise predictable, peaceful lives. The victims are ordinary people killed in the kinds of everyday situations we all find ourselves in. It could have been us—or more frightening, our children—instead of them.

DEATH BY LOTTERY

"This has to be the luckiest day of my life," Harl Partin must have thought. It was Tuesday, March 9, 1976, and as he had done so many times before, the 58-year-old auto worker bought a strip of instant-game Michigan lottery tickets at a grocery store in his Hamtramck neighborhood, then went a few blocks away to Will's Bar to scratch off the numbers.

Partin, a lifelong bachelor only a year away from retirement, spent a lot of free time with his friends at Will's, having a few beers, mostly talking, and sometimes playing cards. He lived just a few steps away in a tiny two-room converted-garage apartment that he rented from the bar's owner, Irene Slabienski.

That Tuesday evening Partin scratched his lotto tickets one by one, tossing each loser in the trash while remarking, "Well, that's life." But suddenly he stared speechless for a few seconds. He had revealed a $10,000 winner. He finally had hit it big, and the excited Partin walked around showing the winning ticket to his pals, while other patrons looked on. Just before the bar closed for the night,

Partin took Slabienski out of sight and sound of the other customers and asked her to lock his winning ticket in the bar's safe. She did, and he left and walked the few yards to his apartment.

Prior to the tavern's opening the next afternoon, a barmaid, accompanied by her children's baby sitter, unlocked the back door of Will's. As they entered, a man with a gun suddenly burst through the door behind them. After locking the two women in the cellar, the man ransacked the cash register and safe, taking $600 and Harl Partin's winning lottery ticket. Slabienski arrived not long after, freed the women, and reported the theft to police.

That evening Partin didn't come into the bar, so at nine o'clock the next morning Slabienski went to his apartment to give him the bad news about his ticket. The door was slightly ajar. Slabienski called out Partin's name, and when he didn't answer, she slowly pushed the door open. The apartment was wrecked. Broken bottles were scattered everywhere, and a mattress covered a heap on the living room floor. Under the mattress Slabienski found Harl Partin's lifeless body.

After an investigation Hamtramck police detectives and Wayne County medical examiners theorized that someone had tied up Partin, then repeatedly beat him with a pool cue and chain to force him to reveal the hiding spot of his $10,000 lottery ticket. When Partin finally gave in, the intruders stuffed a towel into his mouth and tied a pillow case over his head. The attackers had probably not intended to kill Partin, said authorities. But they had bound and gagged the victim in such a manner that he strangled while trying to free himself.

Nearly two weeks later, Alfred Pomaranski, a grocery store owner always on the lookout for creative ways to "make a buck," must have thought it was one of his luckier days. A customer known only as "Charley" walked into Pomaranski's Hamtramck market with a $10,000 winning lottery ticket. The ticket belonged to a "buddy," said Charley, but the friend couldn't cash it himself because he was afraid it would mean an end to his weekly welfare checks. Charley said his anonymous buddy had authorized him to sell the ticket and told Pomaranski he could have it for $7,500. Pomaranski liked the idea but dickered with Charley over the price. They finally settled on $6,500. Pomaranski gave Charley $3,000 and promised to pay him the other $3,500 when he cashed in the ticket. "I figured I'd pay the income tax, give Charley $6,500, and still turn a fast $1,500 for myself," said Pomaranski.

But on March 25, when Pomaranski's wife tried to redeem what turned out to be Harl Partin's stolen ticket at an Oak Park lottery redemption center, the grocer who wanted to turn a quick but questionable profit found himself a murder suspect instead.

Police interrogated the Pomaranskis and Charley, then tracked down Charley's "buddy," a man named Al who said he had, in fact, sold Charley the ticket. Al told police a variety of stories about where he had obtained Partin's ticket. He bought it "for $10 from a man who had bad eyes and thought it was only worth that much." He bought it at a grocery store but couldn't remember which one. He won it in a poker game from a man he didn't know.

In the end the police were unable to connect the Pomaranskis, Charley or Al to Partin's murder and couldn't trace the much-traveled lottery ticket any farther.

Pomaranski persisted in trying to collect the $10,000, reportedly saying, "They'll have to prove to me that the man was murdered over the ticket I bought." But an Oakland Circuit Court judge ruled that the money was stolen property that should be paid to Partin's estate, ultimately to be divided among a brother and four sisters.

Alfred Pomaranski, the last in a list of those who had tried to take a shortcut to lottery luck, was out $3,000. Harl Partin, in a moment of good fortune, had lost his life. And whoever killed him and whoever stole his ticket remains a mystery.

WHERE DID YOU GO, JIMMY HOFFA?

When former Teamsters president Jimmy Hoffa disappeared from the parking lot of a suburban Detroit restaurant in 1975, investigators first treated the case as a search for a missing person, then as a kidnapping. After only a few days, however, there was little doubt as to what had happened to the 62-year-old labor leader. He was murdered.

Who did it, how and why? And — the question that at times seemed paramount to the press and the public — what happened to the body? After nearly 20 years, there are still few definite answers.

There are, however, plenty of allegations, theories and speculations. Most sound so fantastic, so bizarre, they don't seem to be even fictionally possible. But it is perhaps more unrealistic to expect any other kind of ending to the life of a powerful man who juggled relationships with the Mafia, the White House, and possibly the CIA, and who was suspected in assassination plots against a foreign leader and a U.S. president.

Jimmy Hoffa was only 16 when he led his first labor strike, at a Kroger grocery dock in Detroit in the 1930s. Over the next two decades, he fought, often literally, his way to the top of the International Brotherhood of Teamsters. He didn't use just union members to wage his battles. In the 1940s, while involved in a war with a rival union, Hoffa began hiring extra needed muscle from an outside source — organized crime.

After becoming Teamsters president in 1957, Hoffa turned the union into the country's most powerful labor force. He unified the nation's truckers and boosted their wages and benefits. He gathered members of other professions and industries into the Teamsters' fold, usually by bringing welcome support and aid to their strikes and organizing efforts. Hoffa also expanded the unholy alliance between the union and organized crime. In exchange for hired violence, the mob set-up or used Teamsters-controlled industries as a facade of legitimacy.

Hoffa became so powerful that in the 1960s the CIA may have asked him for help in involving the Mafia in a plot to murder Cuban Premier Fidel Castro. And Hoffa became so feared that, immediately after President John F. Kennedy's 1963 assassination, U.S. Attorney General Robert Kennedy and several aides investigated the Teamsters leader's possible involvement in the killing.

Failing to prove any such connection, Robert Kennedy intensified an ongoing Justice Department investigation into alleged fraud and misuse of Teamster pension funds by Hoffa. Finally, in 1967 Jimmy Hoffa was convicted of jury tampering and mail fraud and sentenced to 13 years in a federal prison. Forced to temporarily relinquish his union presidency, Hoffa turned over the leadership of the Teamsters to a "caretaker," Frank Fitzsimmons.

In 1971 President Richard M. Nixon commuted Hoffa's sentence, but with an unprecedented and probably unconstitutional restriction that forbade Hoffa from being involved in union politics until 1980. Upon his release from prison, Hoffa challenged Nixon's order in court and began a fight to regain the union presidency, which Fitzsimmons had decided he would not willingly give up. It appeared likely that Hoffa would win on both fronts.

That possibility unnerved many powerful figures in both the union and the underworld. Hoffa charged that, under the power structure set up by Fitzsimmons, the Teamsters had virtually been taken over by members of organized crime. If he again became the union's president, Hoffa promised to "shake things up." One of his first acts, he said, would be to halt the Fitzsimmons-administration practice of making loans from the union's pension fund to dubious Mafia-controlled businesses.

Especially threatened were the East Coast Teamsters, headed by Anthony "Tony Pro" Provenzano. Provenzano had allegedly risen to power through the ranks of one of the East's major crime families. In the early days, he and Hoffa had been friends. But in the mid-1960s, while both were serving time in the same federal prison, Provenzano and Hoffa had a major falling out and reportedly even got into a fist fight.

As Hoffa waged his battle to enter the 1976 union election, informers said Provenzano was arranging a $9 million pension fund loan to a New Jersey Mafia figure in exchange for a $900,000 kickback. Hoffa's election probably would terminate the deal. On the other hand, Hoffa could not realistically expect to reclaim the union presidency without Provenzano's support.

Throughout early 1975 a mutual friend, Anthony "Tony Jack" Giacalone tried to set up and mediate a "peace meeting" between Hoffa and Provenzano. In late July Giacalone, a reputed powerful figure in Detroit-area organized crime, apparently succeeded.

At about 1 p.m. on July 30, 1975, Jimmy Hoffa pulled on a pair of dark blue slacks and matching sport shirt and left his lakeside home in Orion Township. He told his wife, Josephine, that he was going to meet Giacalone and Provenzano at the Machus Red Fox restaurant, on Telegraph Road near Maple Road in Bloomfield Township. On the way he stopped off at the business of Louis Linteau, a close personal friend and confidant. Linteau was not in, so Hoffa left a message that he was on his way to meet Provenzano and Giacalone.

At 2:30 p.m. Hoffa called Josephine and asked, "Where the hell is Giacalone? He hasn't showed. Has he called?" After Josephine said, "no," Hoffa hung up and went back out into the restaurant parking lot, where several people — including one who shook hands with him — saw him impatiently pacing in the sweltering heat. About an hour later, Louis Linteau picked up his ringing phone. A furious Hoffa bellowed, "The bastards haven't shown up yet."

Nor would they. Provenzano was playing cards 600 miles away, at Local 560 Teamster Union headquarters in Union City, New Jersey. Giacalone was enjoying a massage and a haircut at the Southfield Athletic Club.

Moments after Hoffa had called Linteau, a dark-colored luxury car pulled into the restaurant's parking lot. Jimmy Hoffa got in and vanished.

Hoffa's disappearance launched one of the most intensive and sensational manhunts in the nation's history. The investigation ultimately involved tracking dogs, hundreds of FBI agents, thousands of interviews, bumper stickers, reward money, hypnosis, lineups, grand juries, grants of immunity and changed identities. But two decades later, there have been no convictions, no prosecutions, not a single arrest for the murder of Jimmy Hoffa.

While the case lacks significant physical evidence and solid leads, there is no shortage of theories.

— A Chicago underworld hit man said the CIA ordered Hoffa killed so that he couldn't reveal the details of the agency's 1960s plot to assassinate Fidel Castro.

— Joe Franco, a self-proclaimed confidant of Hoffa's, also suspects government involvement. In his book, *Hoffa's Man* (Dell Publishing Co., 1987), Franco made the astonishing claim that, from his car at a distance, he accidentally witnessed Hoffa's abduction by three men who dressed like "federal agents." After the men flashed official-looking identification, Hoffa got into their black Lincoln, which Franco said he followed until it turned off toward a Pontiac airport.

— In the November 1989 issue of *Playboy* magazine, Donald "Tony the Greek" Frankos said he told the FBI that two members of an Irish mob killed Hoffa in a house near Mt. Clemens. Frankos, who said he was a federally protected mob informant, claimed he was supposed to participate in the killing but couldn't because he was in prison.

— Charles Allen, an admitted Mafia enforcer who was Jimmy Hoffa's bodyguard in prison, told a U.S. Senate subcommittee that he had been ordered by Hoffa to kill his rivals, Frank Fitzsimmons and Tony Provenzano. Allen, who had been given a new identity in a federal witness protection program, testified that Hoffa was then killed on orders from Fitzsimmons and Provenzano after they learned of the plot.

— *Time* magazine reported in a November 1977 issue that Gino Gallina, a reputed Mafia attorney gunned down gangland fashion in New York, had hidden a tape recording of mobsters talking about their first-hand role in Hoffa's killing. Investigators conducted a search, including a safe deposit box rented by Gallina under an assumed name, but found no such tape.

The FBI says they *know* who killed Jimmy Hoffa and why. According to the "HOFFEX Memo" (a summary of the FBI investigation) Tony Provenzano, with the approval of Mafia higher-ups, ordered Hoffa killed to ensure that the East Coast Teamsters/mob empire would not be destroyed by a change in union leadership and policies. Three of Provenzano's New Jersey colleagues flew into town and carried out the hit, says the report.

The trio was taken to the Machus Red Fox, according to the FBI, in a car driven by 41-year-old Charles "Chuckie" O'Brien. O'Brien, the son of a close Hoffa family friend, had been virtually raised by Hoffa and, in fact, was often referred to as the union leader's "foster son." But the pair recently had had intense personal and business disagreements. Still, O'Brien was one of the few people Hoffa would trust enough to enter a car. Hoffa got in, probably thinking he was finally going to the meeting with Provenzano and Giacalone. O'Brien — knowingly or as an unwitting dupe, the FBI says they aren't sure — then chauferred Jimmy Hoffa to the place where he was murdered, a red-brick colonial style house just two miles from the Red Fox.

O'Brien has steadfastly denied his involvement. But several witnesses reported seeing O'Brien driving a maroon 1975 Mercury in the vicinity of the Red Fox shortly before Hoffa disappeared. When the FBI examined the car, which O'Brien had borrowed from Tony Giacalone's son, they found bits of hair matching Hoffa's. And three different tracking dogs detected Hoffa's scent on both the right rear seat and in the trunk.

But, said Special Agent John Anthony of the FBI in Detroit, "What we do not know with a degree of certainty is the disposition of his body."

The agency may not know, but thousands of others — including those who identified themselves as psychics, witches, private investigators, astrological advisors, mystics, and underworld informants — said they did. The FBI, in fact, received so many "tips" about the location of Hoffa's body that they finally had to issue a news release stating that it was a federal crime to deliberately furnish false leads.

According to some of the more-fascinating, sometimes-credible theories, Jimmy Hoffa's body was

— buried on a 29-acre farm field in Waterford Township 11 miles northwest of the Red Fox restaurant. So said a "reliable" informant, who told a U.S. Senate committee investigating organized crime that he had helped bury the body. Based on the tip, State Attorney General Frank Kelley, two federal investigators, and 25 state and local police officers descended on the field on September 28, 1975. While hundreds of spectators watched, the men dug with backhoes and hand shovels for several days but did not uncover Hoffa's grave.

— mashed into unrecognizable pieces in a large, orange trash compacter behind the Raleigh House, a Tudor style catering hall in Southfield, just a three-minute drive from the Red Fox.

— stuffed into a 50-gallon oil drum, trucked across the country, and buried in a muddy 37-acre dump in Hudson County, New Jersey.

— cut up, placed in black plastic bags, stored in a freezer for several months, then placed in a large oil drum and carted from Michigan to the East Rutherford, New Jersey, site where Giants Stadium was under construction. The remains were buried in concrete underneath what is now Section 107 near the end zone.

— cremated in an industrial waste incinerator in Hamtramck.

— weighted and dropped from a private plane into the middle of one of the Great Lakes.

— reduced to pulp in a mammoth paper shredder at Central Sanitation Services in Hamtramck.

— encased in concrete and dumped off Key West, Florida.

—taken to New Jersey where it was ground up at an ironworks, stuffed into a steel drum, transported to Florida, and dumped in the Everglades.

— mixed with concrete being used at any of several metro-Detroit construction sites.

— dissolved in a vat of molten zinc at a Detroit metal-plating company.

— placed in a junk car that was then crushed and smelted.

Whatever was done with Jimmy Hoffa's body, his killers made sure it would never be found.

With no body and only circumstantial evidence, the FBI said they couldn't make arrests until someone who planned or carried out the murder confessed or agreed to testify. In spite of promises of immunity, changed identities and relocation, only one of the suspected key figures ever appeared ready to accept the offer. And he was immediately slain, "mob-style," as an evidently effective warning to others.

Year after year, one by one, others who probably know what happened to Hoffa also die, either of natural causes or by violent means.

The FBI says the investigation is officially still open. But unless one of the few remaining principals in the case breaks the code of silence or makes a deathbed confession, there will be no solution to one of the most celebrated crimes of this century.

DYING IN PARADISE

For more than a century, millions of tourists have ferried over to Mackinac Island to enjoy the unique blend of history, scenery and shopping.

For one visitor, however, the beautiful, world-famous vacation spot turned into a deadly getaway. On July 24, 1960, 49-year-old Frances Lacey became the only tourist ever to be murdered while visiting Mackinac Island. The Dearborn woman was killed on a weekend during the peak of the tourist season, at a time when the island was packed with people. She was slain in broad daylight along the main road that circles the shore of the island, a road that is usually busy with tourists riding bicycles or in carriages. Yet no one witnessed the slaying or saw the killer, and the murder has never been solved.

Lacey, her daughter and son-in-law arrived on the island together on Saturday morning for a two-day, one-night stay. Lacey checked into her room at the Murray Hotel, in the busy "downtown" area, and her daughter and daughter's husband moved into a log cottage they had rented at British Landing, on the opposite, relatively isolated side of the island.

The family then joined 8,000 other "fudgies," as tourists are called, spending the day enjoying Mackinac's many attractions. By early evening Lacey was pleasantly exhausted from the first day of the first vacation she had taken since her husband's death more than two years before. She retired to her hotel room after telling her daughter she planned to walk to their cottage the next morning and to expect her about 11.

Lacey slept soundly awoke early and slipped on an aquamarine skirt, white blouse, and gray canvas walking shoes. After a solitary 8 a.m. breakfast, she returned to her hotel room, where she placed a pair of blue dress shoes she planned to wear when she got to her daughter's cabin into a plastic bag. She neatly packed a few other articles of clothing into a brown suitcase and went to the lobby to check out. Because she had paid for her room in advance, she placed her room key on the registration counter and set her lone suitcase down near the hotel's baggage pickup area.

Shortly after 9 a.m., plastic shoe bag in one hand and purse in the other, Lacey left the lobby of the Murray Hotel and set out to hike the 3¹/₂ miles to British Landing. A few bicyclists and horse-drawn carriages were already on the move as she made her way south past the false Victorian fronts of the fudge outlets, gift shops, hotels and other buildings that line the island's main street. As she turned west around Windemere Point, she carefully made her way along a section of deteriorating boardwalk and then stepped onto Lake Shore Road, an 8-mile ribbon of blacktop that skirts the Lake Huron shoreline around the entire island. She glanced at the Grand Hotel, perched high atop the bluff to her right, then quickened her pace as she entered one of the most thickly wooded, least-visited sections of the well-traveled island.

At about 10 a.m. Lacey sat down to rest near a fieldstone-walled gate about halfway between the Murray Hotel and British Landing. A dirt two-track behind the entranceway led nearly half a mile through the woods to a 60-year-old English-style mansion known as the Stonecliff Estate. At the time the facility served as a summer retreat for Moral Re-Armament, a world-wide fundamentalist Christian organization. Lacey took off her walking shoes and looked out over the cold, gray waters of Lake Huron. Ferries carrying the day's first batches of tourists from Mackinaw City and St. Ignace moved across a backdrop dominated by the nearly new Mackinac Bridge.

The soothing scene was interrupted by the snap of someone stepping on a dead branch behind Lacey. As she stood up and spun around, an unknown man hit her in the face with his fist. The blow knocked her nearly unconscious and sent a partial dental plate flying from her mouth onto the roadway. Lacey dropped her purse but hung onto the plastic shoe bag as the assailant dragged her several yards up a steep incline covered by a tangled thicket of evergreens. Before Lacey regained full consciousness, the man sexually assaulted her and then strangled her with her own panties.

The killer then returned to the roadway, removed a wallet from Lacey's purse, picked up her walking shoes, walked across the road, and threw the canvas oxfords into the water, only a few yards away. He then returned to Lacey's body, picked it up, carried it farther into the woods, and dumped it under a wind-fallen balsam tree about 200 feet from the gate. He threw the bag containing Lacey's dress shoes under a rotting rowboat and began covering her body with tree branches.

The killer, however, had left Lacey's purse lying on the shoulder of the road. As he was busy hiding the body, a couple on a tandem bike stopped, picked up the purse, and carried it away with them. Less than a minute later, another couple in a surrey rode by. The horses' hooves and carriage wheels crunched the dead woman's dental plate into the blacktop. As the clip-clop sounds faded into the distance, the killer fled up a wooded path called Tranquil Lane.

When Lacey's daughter hadn't seen or heard from her mother by noon, she contacted the island police station. During the next few days, the longstanding serenity of Mackinac Island was interrupted by the tense energy of a massive search for the missing woman. On Monday dozens of state and local law enforcement personnel plus nearly a hundred state park employees, Coast Guardsmen, Boy Scouts, area firemen, and volunteer vacationers fanned out on foot, bicycle and horseback. They covered every mile of the vast network of dirt roads and foot trails that criss-cross the 1,700-acre island. Meanwhile, planes and helicopters skimmed over the treetops of heavily wooded areas, and skin divers searched the surrounding waters. On Tuesday the baying of two bloodhounds cut through the morning mist and fog. The tracking dogs twice picked up Lacey's trail and twice lost it.

But after three days the only evidence that Lacey had ever been on the island was the small brown suitcase she had left at the Murray Hotel and her empty wallet, which searchers had found in a hedge near the Grand Hotel.

Then, investigators got a welcome break. The couple who had picked up Lacey's purse from the side of the road had taken it for a reason. When they had looked inside, they found identification that listed Lacey's Dearborn address. The couple who found the purse were also from the Detroit area. Thinking the purse was lost and that it would be much quicker and more convenient for Lacey to get it directly from them, they took it back home and then unsuccessfully tried calling Lacey on Monday night. By Wednesday they had read newspaper accounts of Lacey's disappearance and had notified local police. When turning over the purse, they also told authorities exactly where they had found it — by the stone-walled gate, the only such structure on that side of the island.

On Thursday State Police officers thoroughly examined the area. They quickly discovered pieces of Lacey's dental plate ground into the tar, and they also found one of Lacey's walking shoes, which had floated ashore nearby. But the killer had hidden the body well, and it wasn't until shortly after 7 p.m. on Thursday that investigators discovered the remains of Frances Lacey.

Police had a murder victim but no evidence or clues as to who might have committed the crime. A 25-man force of State Police investigators set out to try and find a homicidal needle in a massive, human haystack. More than 8,000 tourists and 2,000 itinerant workers had been on the island the day Lacey was murdered. Most of the visitors were long gone.

Investigators narrowed the field of suspects somewhat with the theory that whoever had committed the murder had stayed on the island Saturday night. Otherwise, since the first ferry reached the island at 8 a.m., the killer would have had to step off the boat and rush directly to the murder site, about two miles from the ferry docks. Police also figured the killer — whether worker or tourist — had left the island soon after the crime. Authorities investigated every visitor who had checked out of a hotel and every employee who had quit his job on either July 24 and 25. They also checked each person who had rented a bicycle, saddle horse or horse-drawn carriage in the hours prior to the slaying. They came up with no strong suspects.

Some long-time island residents had an even more-specific theory. The murderer, they speculated, was someone "unstable" who was one of several hundred guests at a weekend Moral Re-Armament conference. The killer, according to their scenario, made his way down from Stonecliff, assaulted and strangled Lacey, then left the island with the rest of the group.

After questioning more than 400 persons, including Moral Re-Armament's leaders, and checking out thousands of tips, the State Police essentially threw up their hands in frustration. "We could check on people who worked or lived (on the island) or who were registered in hotels," said the lieutenant who headed the investigation. "But 7,000 other tourists were on the island that Sunday. How could we check on all of them?"

Whoever murdered Frances Lacey was never caught and probably never again returned to Mackinac Island. If he did, he never killed again.

SILENCING A SENATOR

Forty-year-old state Senator Warren G. Hooper most likely didn't realize what was happening to him. Someone grabbed the brim of his fedora and yanked it down over his eyes with such force that it tore the brim. A .38-caliber bullet from a long-barreled Colt revolver then smashed squarely into the left side of the Albion man's balding head, killing him instantly. The lifeless hand of the chain smoker dropped his last cigarette onto the seat between his legs. As Hooper's slim body slumped toward the dash of his 1939 Mercury, his slayer fired a second and third shot into his skull at such close range they left powder burns on the hat.

The assailant then calmly walked from Hooper's car — marking the freshly fallen snow with footprints from the driver's door around the front of the car — and got into a waiting getaway vehicle.

Ten minutes later, at about 5:30 p.m., two men driving by on rural M-99 3¹/₂ miles north of Springport found the car and Hooper's body, with flames from a carseat fire started by the burning cigarette rising between the corpse's legs. The men threw in snow to put out the blaze, then dragged Hooper's body out into the cold darkness of that Thursday, January 11, 1945, night.

Soon after, police arrived and started a murder investigation that, over the next 45 years, would raise far more questions than it answered.

Michigan residents were shocked by the killing. But some weren't surprised, including Hooper's wife, Callienetta, and special prosecutor Kim Sigler. Hooper was scheduled to be a star witness in Sigler's grand jury probe of legislative corruption. When the lawmaker told his wife that he, in effect, was going to cross and possibly send to prison some of the most powerful men in the state, Callienetta warned, "Warren, your life isn't worth a penny. Not a penny."

Since the 1920s rumors had circulated throughout the state, but especially in Lansing, that "special interests" could buy votes to influence every kind of legislation. The corruption, in fact, was real. And when it got so bad that lobbyists began placing money and notes of instruction in the pockets of legislators' overcoat pockets hanging in the capitol cloakroom, the state attorney general, in late 1943, finally set up an investigation.

It took the form of a one-man grand jury in the person of 60-year-old Ingham County Circuit Court Senior Judge Leland W. Carr. Carr selected as his special prosecutor a flamboyant, 49-year-old Battle Creek attorney named Kim Sigler. A year later Sigler and Carr had succeeded in convicting 24 people, including past and present state legislators, in a bribery plot. But Sigler was frustrated in his failure to indict the more-powerful figures he felt certain were responsible for the corruption.

At the top of Sigler's "hit list" was Frank McKay. A script writer or novelist would have had a hard time inventing a character that better portrayed a "political boss" than McKay. The self-made real estate magnate from Grand Rapids served two terms as state treasurer. After leaving office in 1931, McKay took absolute control of the Michigan Republican Party, personally selecting Republican candidates for major state offices, then bankrolling their campaigns. By most accounts McKay wielded his power well beyond ethical and legal limits. Throughout his political career, grand juries several times had linked him to illegal gambling, extortion, conflict of interest and influence peddling. But no one had ever successfully prosecuted him.

Intent on being the first, Sigler methodically set out to interrogate every legislator. When Warren Hooper's turn came, he cracked under Sigler's relentless questioning and blurted that he had been given money from McKay in return for a favorable vote on upcoming legislation.

Shortly after, in an unusual and fateful move, Sigler stood Hooper in the same room as McKay and two of McKay's assistants and made the shaking first-term senator repeat his charges. Sigler was gambling on an easy way out — that faced with the certainty of Hooper's damning testimony, at least one of the three would confess. But when Hooper named one of the assistants as the man from whom he had received money, all three just stared silently back at him. Having broken the confidentiality of the investigation without success, Sigler pressed on. On December 2, 1944, he served conspiracy warrants on McKay and his two assistants. And he scheduled Warren Hooper to officially testify on Monday, January 15, 1945.

Shortly after 4 p.m. on the 11th, Hooper got into his green Mercury, lit a cigarette, and headed from Lansing for a restful weekend with his wife and two young sons, ages four and six, at their Albion home. A little more than an hour later, he was dead.

State Police investigators found few clues — partial prints of three fingers of a left hand on the driver's door, a partial palm print on the left rear door, and the tracks in the snow. Skid marks indicated that Hooper's car had stopped quickly, but under control. A 6-inch scrape of maroon paint marred the right fender of Hooper's green car.

Based on that evidence, police theorized that the killer — either someone Hooper knew or someone who had abducted him — had driven Hooper's car, quickly pulled off the side of the road, shot the senator, then got into a maroon car that had followed.

State Police weren't the only ones investigating the crime. With his key witness dead, Kim Sigler was forced to drop his bribery case against McKay. Instead, the special prosecutor focused his energy on not only solving Hooper's murder but also connecting McKay to it.

After spending nearly two and a half months of fruitlessly checking out hundreds of clues and leads, investigators finally made a breakthrough. Under interrogation two ex-cons said they had been hired to kill Hooper, whom they said had to be "taken care of" before he testified. They had even gone to Albion twice but, because Hooper wasn't alone, couldn't "finish the job." Somebody else obviously had, but the two said they didn't know who.

They did know who put up the $15,000 for the contract, however, but it wasn't Frank McKay. They said it was Sam Fleisher, acting head of Detroit's notorious Purple Gang, which had achieved underworld supremacy during the Prohibition era. Based on the pair of ex-convicts' testimony, for which they were granted immunity, Fleisher and three other men were convicted of conspiring to kill Warren Hooper. Thirty minutes after being found guilty, the judge sentenced each to the maximum prison terms allowed — five years.

They served their terms without saying then, or ever, if they knew who pulled the trigger or who paid to have it done.

In March 1946, under a political barrage of criticism for his questionable handling of grand jury expenditures, Kim Sigler was fired as special prosecutor. A week and a half later, he announced his candidacy for governor on the Republican ticket, and in November the man who had attained immense popularity in his crime-busting role as special prosecutor was elected Michigan's 40th governor.

Sigler vowed to continue his pursuit of Hooper's killer, but one of his first acts as Michigan's new chief executive was to replace the 21-year-veteran State Police director who had diligently and effectively supervised the investigation. Sigler appointed Donald Leonard, then turned his attention to more politically pressing and popular matters.

Sigler was defeated for re-election in 1948, and when he left office, he took all of his records of the Hooper case with him. When Donald Leonard resigned in 1952, he, too, took all State Police records of the investigation into the Hooper murder, and the probe officially ended. A year later Kim Sigler died in a plane crash, and the murder and its investigation began to fade from memory.

The Hooper killing might have completed its fall from headlines to historical footnote, except for the efforts of two professors, Lawrence E. Ziewacz of Michigan State University and Bruce A. Rubenstein of the University of Michigan-Flint.

In an extraordinary five-year research effort in the mid-1980s, the pair pieced together evidence investigators at the time were not able to. These included secret grand jury transcripts, the files taken by Leonard and Sigler, and transcripts of interviews with convicts and Purple Gang members.

Their research complete, Rubenstein and Ziewacz said they knew who had murdered Warren Hooper and named the killers in their book, *Three Bullets Sealed His Lips* (Michigan State University Press, 1987). Their stranger-than-fiction theory in abbreviated form:

Corruption at the time of Hooper's murder was not limited to the capital. An investigation by the Michigan Attorney General revealed that "favored" Jackson Prison inmates, such as former Purple Gang leaders, were regularly able to buy their way out of that institution for a few hours. The prison staff even furnished the inmates with civilian clothes and vehicles for their excursions, usually drinking and carousing at Detroit bars.

During one such trip, two inmates — Purple Gang members hired by Frank McKay through a series of intermediaries, including Sam Fleisher — drove the short distance to M-99, forced Hooper's car off the road, shot the senator, then returned to the prison. The carefully planned killing, the authors say, was carried out with the full knowledge and even the help of the Jackson Prison warden and with the use of the deputy warden's maroon car.

Perhaps more shocking, say Rubenstein and Ziewacz, Kim Sigler, too, knew who had killed Hooper. But by maintaining strict control over the inquiry and allowing various investigators only pieces of evidence, he deliberately did not solve the murder because he could not involve his ultimate target, Frank McKay.

Two years after the authors' claim that Sigler, even while governor, had deliberately prevented the solution to Hooper's murder, the State Police briefly reopened the investigation. According to Rubenstein the police found nothing to dispute his and Ziewacz's conclusions, but they also found nothing with which they could proceed further.

Officially, Warren Hooper's murder remains unsolved.

CREAM OR SUGAR?

Marga Stya said she didn't feel well and excused herself to the restroom. A few minutes later when she returned to the restaurant booth where her husband and four other friends waited, she could barely walk. She also felt dizzy, she said, and was having trouble breathing. Her husband helped her lie down on the padded seats and tried to comfort her while one of the friends called for an ambulance. By the time Marga Stya, a healthy 43-year-old triathlete, reached Detroit Samaritan Health Center 30 minutes later, she was dead.

Stya's sudden, unexpected death was a shocking end to a 1989 holiday season that had been particularly joyous for her and her husband, Allen Scafuri. After a nearly four-year cross-country commuter marriage, they were finally preparing to be permanently together. Stya, a research scientist, had left Michigan in 1985 to become vice president of a Seattle, Washington, research laboratory. Scafuri stayed behind as a visiting professor of economics at Wayne State University, and the couple spent as much time together as they could at their Farmington Hills condominium. In 1989 Scafuri was thrilled to obtain a teaching position at the University of Washington in Seattle. He and Marga would finally be together. Stya flew home for the holidays and spent the week after Christmas helping her husband get ready for the move.

The afternoon of December 31, Stya ran in the Little Caesars Pizza New Years Eve four-mile "fun run" on Belle Isle. After the race, at about 5:30, she, her husband, and four friends went to a nearby restaurant on East Jefferson. Stya ordered only a coffee and poured in two packets of powdered non-dairy creamer and one of sugar. Between bursts of animated conversation, she drank the coffee and picked at a piece of pie her husband had ordered. An hour later, she was dead.

The Wayne County Medical Examiner's office was asked to investigate the mysterious death. When an autopsy revealed no evidence of trauma or death by natural causes, toxicology tests were ordered. For a moment the unexpected results surprised even the medical examiner. Stya was killed by a lethal dose of cyanide. Suicide was quickly ruled out. Her death, the medical examiner ruled, was a homicide.

Who had fed Stya the fatal poison, why and how? Because cyanide, which attacks the body's central nervous system, is very fast-acting, Stya had to have ingested it while at the restaurant, said the medical examiner. Stya occasionally took medication for her allergies, and investigators first suspected that her over-the-counter antihistamine tablets may have been laced with the poison. But the medical examiner's report showed she had not recently taken medication of any kind, and tests on Stya's supply of tablets revealed no presence of cyanide.

Investigators next focused on what Stya ate and drank. She had sampled only a few small bites of her husband's pie. He had eaten the rest and did not get sick. All six people at her booth had drunk coffee poured from the same pitcher, but again, no one else felt even slightly ill. And with six people squeezed into the booth, it would have been nearly impossible for someone sitting with Stya or a passerby to have surreptitiously slipped something into her coffee cup.

Stya, however, was the only one in her group who had added the small institutional packets of creamer and sugar to her coffee. Everyone else had drunk theirs black. Inspectors from the Detroit Health Department, however, found no evidence of tampering with the restaurant's coffee, cream or sugar supply.

Had someone randomly added cyanide to a single packet of creamer or sugar before it was shipped to the restaurant? Was Marga Stya simply in the wrong place at the wrong time, unknowingly involved in Russian roulette a la carte? Could a previous occupant or the next person in the booth have been the random victim? Or *was* Stya somehow, for some reason singled out by someone at the restaurant?

The investigating homicide detective vowed to find out, even if "it took the rest of my career." However, in the absence of any solid leads, witnesses, apparent motive, or hard evidence of any kind, the file was soon set aside and later lost.

Whoever was responsible for Marga Stya's death may have committed the perfect crime.

THE BABY SITTER

February 15, 1976 — Mark Stebbins, 12, was playing games with friends at the Ferndale American Legion Hall when around noon he said he was going home to watch television. He never arrived. Four days later his body was found neatly laid out in funereal position in a snowbank next to a Southfield office building.

December 22, 1976 — After an argument with her mother, 12-year-old Jill Robinson stormed out of her Royal Oak home and walked to a nearby hobby shop. Four days later her body was found on I-75 north of 16-Mile Road in Troy. Again, the killer had carefully placed the body, funeral style, in the snow.

January 2, 1977 — Kristine Mihelich, 10, left her home in Berkley and walked three blocks to a convenience store, where she bought a teen magazine. She didn't return home. Nearly three weeks later, a mail carrier found her body alongside a lonely road in Franklin Village. Mihelich had suffered the same ritualistic end as Stebbins and Robinson. Her abductor had fed, bathed, groomed — including a manicure and pedicure — and dressed her in freshly washed and pressed clothing before suffocating her. The killer then carefully laid out her body on its back, hands folded over the chest, in a snowbank.

Apprehension rippled through Detroit's affluent northern suburbs. The bizarre and baffling murders, all of which began or ended in

Oakland County, appeared to be the work of one ritualistic psychopath. On January 21, 1977, the same day Mihelich's body was discovered, personnel from 13 area police departments organized into a task force led by the Michigan State Police. The team began its hunt for a killer macabrely called "the baby sitter" because of the great care and attention that had been lavished on the victims during their several-day stay with the slayer.

The investigation had barely begun when, on March 16, 1977, 12-year-old Timothy King borrowed 30 cents from his older sister and, with his ever-present orange skateboard in hand, left his Birmingham home and walked to a shopping center five blocks away. After buying three candy bars at a drugstore, he left through the store's rear door, which opened to a parking lot, and disappeared. Six days later his body, dressed in freshly laundered and pressed blue pants and red jacket, was found gently laid out in a shallow ditch along a rural Livonia road. Carefully placed next to King's body was his orange skateboard. King, like the three other slain children, had been smothered. There was no doubt the "baby sitter" had claimed a fourth victim.

The ripple of anxiety surged to a wave of fear, and Oakland County's streets became eerily absent of children. Parents took students to and from their schools in a traffic-choking procession of vehicles. The few children who did walk traveled in pairs and under the watchful eyes of parents stationed along the routes. Schools called home to verify every absence, and parents called schools if their children were even a few minutes late coming home. Bicycles no longer lined up outside favorite sub-teen hangouts, and children even avoided playing in a park behind the Birmingham police station.

Policemen, psychologists and social workers visited nearly every elementary classroom in a 13-community area with instructions on what to do if approached by a friendly stranger. And place mats at a fast food restaurant, milk cartons in a supermarket, T-shirts and bumper stickers all featured "don't talk to strangers" warnings.

With the murder of Timothy King, the investigation escalated to become the most intensive manhunt ever conducted in Michigan. At its peak the task force included nearly 200 full-time investigators, detectives and civilian workers from 18 police agencies.

But they had little to go on. There was no apparent motive behind the slayings and, because the killer had immaculately cleaned the victims' bodies and clothes, no evidence.

There may have been witnesses, however, who caught a glimpse of the killer. Two shoppers who had been in the parking lot where Timothy King had disappeared told police they had seen the boy talking to a man in a blue Gremlin. Investigators ultimately questioned every Gremlin owner in Oakland County, but all were exonerated. From the witnesses' descriptions, police drew and released a composite sketch of a dark-complected white male, 25-35 years old, with a shag haircut and bushy sideburns.

Authorities also put together a psychological/personality profile. The killer, they determined, was probably well-educated and held a white-collar or professional job that gave him freedom of movement. He was average in size and appearance and thus wouldn't be particularly noticeable. He was intelligent, quiet and polite and may have appeared to be a person children would trust and go with willingly, such as a doctor, a policeman, or a member of the clergy. Investigators also said the baby sitter was intimately familiar with Oakland County and lived in a place where he could keep children without arousing suspicion.

One psychiatrist who worked closely with the task force may have come agonizingly close to finding out the baby sitter's identity. Just a few weeks after Timothy King's murder, the doctor received a letter from a man named "Allen," who said not only did he share an apartment with the murderer, but also had helped look after the victims in the days before they were killed. Allen claimed his roommate had been traumatized by killing children in Vietnam and wanted to make the "rich people" who had sent him to war suffer as he had.

Allen also phoned the doctor and offered to trade proof in the form of Polaroid pictures for a grant of immunity from prosecution. The FBI and other experts determined that Allen's letter and phone call were probably genuine, so the psychiatrist made arrangements to meet Allen in a bar near Woodward and Seven Mile. But Allen never showed up and was never seen or heard from again, leaving authorities to speculate that the baby sitter may have also murdered his roommate/accomplice.

The task force investigators spent almost two years checking out more than 18,000 other tips and leads. They interviewed half a dozen people under hypnosis and even called in a New York pyschic and a team of university experts in cult murders. But every avenue of approach led to a dead end, and on December 15, 1978, the task force officially ended its investigation.

The baby sitter, too, ended his killing spree, and the police wonder why. They hope he is dead, perhaps committing suicide after being overwhelmed by guilt. Some think he may have left the area, afraid that he would be caught, but no similar ritualistic killings of children were subsequently reported anywhere else in the country. Others speculate that the murderer came from a well-to-do family who might have sent him out of the country for psychiatric treatment or even gotten him committed to an institution. The family name would be protected, the man would receive treatment, and the family could be assured no one else would be killed.

One frightening possibility is that the child killer might be in prison as the result of some other comparatively minor crime. If so, one day he likely will be released and may again stalk some community's children.

FINAL RESTING PLACE

As Jane Snow headed her car up I-75 during the early evening hours of Tuesday, May 15, 1979, she reveled in the relaxation of not having to battle weekend "up north" traffic for a change. And as she pulled off at one of the freeway's rest areas, it struck her how unusual it was that she and her family would even have that normally busy facility to themselves. Jane Snow's assessment turned out to be dead wrong.

Snow and her two sons — Eric, 9, and Mark, 7 — were making the familiar but long drive from their Grand Rapids home to Escanaba, where Snow's parents lived. The boys were looking forward to spending four days with their grandparents, and Snow was relieved that this would be her next-to-last such trip. The 31-year-old registered nurse, divorced for four years, had resigned her position at a Grand Rapids hospital effective June 1 and planned to move to

Escanaba at that time. The purpose of this trip was to finalize living arrangements.

At around 7:30 p.m., three hours after leaving home, Snow eased her five-year-old Dodge Dart off north I-75 and into the Loon Lake rest area, just south of Gaylord. Snow and her sons walked into the facility — Jane to the women's restroom and Mark and Eric to the men's. The two boys came out and, not seeing their mother, went outside and let the family's dog out of the car. While they played with the animal on the grass, they saw no other cars pull into the paved lot nor anyone leave or enter the building.

After about 10 minutes, when his mother still had not come out of the building, Mark went inside to check. He stood at the restroom door and called. When he heard no answer, he stepped inside to find his mother lying in a huge pool of blood on the cold, cement floor. Either shielded by innocence or shocked into composure, the little boy knelt next to his mother's body and pulled a quarter out of her purse. He then stepped into the lobby, put the coin into the pay telephone, and dialed "0". But the phone didn't work, so Mark ran outside past his surprised brother and onto I-75, where he forced a car to squeal to a stop.

The surprised occupants, a married couple from Wolverine, heard Mark sob, "Mommy's hurt," and rushed into the rest area to help. The woman comforted the two boys while her husband, after feeling no pulse on Jane Snow's wrist, tried calling the police from the rest area's pay phone. Unable to use the phone, he ran out onto I-75 and flagged down a car, whose driver rushed to the Gaylord State Police post. An hour after Jane Snow had pulled into the peaceful, wooded rest area for a routine stop, a state trooper arrived to examine her cold, lifeless body. An autopsy the next morning revealed that someone had stabbed her 23 times with a double-edged knife.

But who? It was obvious the killer did not know Jane Snow. Only a few close friends and family members were aware that she was making the trip north. And because the stop at Loon Lake wasn't planned or timed, no one could have known if she would use that particular facility. Also, she had not been sexually attacked or robbed, so it appeared to be a random, motiveless slaying.

And whoever committed the murder had entered the rest area on foot and left the same way, without being seen. Several people, upon reading or hearing reports of the killing, called State Police to say they had seen only Snow's brown Dodge or no cars at the rest area as they had driven by on I-75 during times immediately preceding and following the murder. And neither passersby nor Mark or Eric Snow had seen any other person on the rest area grounds.

For several days following the killing, investigators carefully inspected the rest area from the top of the building to the bottom of nearby Loon Lake, and tracking dogs sniffed the grounds, the freeway shoulders, and the surrounding woods. But after four days of searching, all that was found was a bloody footprint on the restroom floor and two matching prints in the dirt outside.

State Police had little evidence, but they did have an immediate suspect, a 28-year-old unemployed "drifter" named John McGawley. On the day of the murder, McGawley had spent the afternoon bar-hopping his way from Onaway back toward Gaylord. Employees at taverns in Onaway, Tower, Afton, Indian River and Wolverine reported that they had quit serving McGawley because he was acting "crazy" or "bizarre." At about 6:30 p.m., after being cut off at a bar in Indian River, McGawley walked out to the on-ramp from M-68 to I-75, stuck out his thumb, and soon hitched a ride. The bartender later discovered that a knife used to slice onions near where John McGawley had been sitting was missing.

An hour later, within minutes of the knifing of Jane Snow, a state trooper pulled his unmarked patrol car onto the shoulder of southbound I-75 next to a man signaling for rides. The officer told the man he could not hitch-hike on the expressway and asked him for identification. It was John McGawley, and he and the trooper were standing almost directly across the freeway from the Loon Lake rest area.

The officer, not knowing that Jane Snow lay dead or dying less than 200 yards away, frisked McGawley and, finding no weapons, ordered him into the patrol car. The trooper then drove McGawley nine miles south to the nearest exit and let him out. As the officer watched while having supper in a nearby restaurant, McGawley thumbed a ride and got into a vehicle that headed down the on-ramp and onto south I-75. When the trooper got back into his car, he received a request over his radio to provide assistance to an officer involved the homicide at the Loon Lake rest area.

Only hours after Snow's murder was reported, State Police picked up McGawley at the Pontiac address listed on his suspended driver's license, which had been recorded by the trooper who had picked him up. McGawley denied having anything to do with Snow's murder and allowed investigators to analyze his clothing as well as blood and hair samples and fingernail scrapings. He also submitted to two polygraph examinations. The polygraphs and lab tests on the McGawley's clothing and body tissues turned up nothing conclusive.

The only "evidence" to connect McGawley to Snow's brutal killing was his presence near the murder scene and the fact that footprints from his shoes were similar to those found at the rest area. But if McGawley had committed the murder, he would have had to quickly make his way from the rest area building across both northbound and southbound lanes of I-75 without being noticed and then stand there calmly as though nothing had happened. And somehow, somewhere on the way he would have had to get rid of the murder weapon where no one would find it.

Lacking any hard evidence, police released McGawley and concentrated on a second suspect, a man whose home was separated from the rest area by only a half mile of woods and I-75. During the weeks before the murder, Gaylord police had received several complaints that the 30-year-old man, already on probation for an arson offense, was following women home from a local restaurant. One of the suspect's two former wives also told police that, on several occasions during their marriage, he had gone "beserk" and beaten her. When investigators questioned the man, he said he had never walked through the woods to Loon Lake and had spent the night of the murder doing yard work and watching television.

In January 1980 the man married again, but after only a few months, his third wife also left him. The woman then reported to police that, not long after the wedding, she had overheard her husband's mother tell him she knew he had been "for a walk in the woods" the night of the murder and that he'd better not let police find out. The suspect's young daughter by his first marriage, who was temporarily living with the couple at the time, said that she, too, had heard the conversation. Still, police could find nothing substantive to connect the man to Snow's murder.

During the next two years, police continued to receive tips, but the last entry in the case file is dated May 18, 1982, three years almost exactly to the day Jane Snow died. Officially the investigation is ongoing. Unofficially it's over.

Jane Snow had every expectation of making a routine stop and continuing on her way. Instead she encountered someone who did get away . . . with murder.

PRESCRIPTION FOR MURDER?

For six weeks during July and August 1975 an epidemic of respiratory failures swept through the Veterans Administration Hospital in Ann Arbor. Nearly half the 52 stricken patients experienced the same unusual symptom — a sudden, unexpected sensation of hands gripping their lungs and relentlessly squeezing — which left them unable to breathe without mechanical aid. Some victims suffered the strange attacks more than once. Twelve died.

The alarming number and mysterious nature of the breathing failures caused patients and staff alike to wonder if a psychopathic killer ran loose in the hospital. An FBI investigation confirmed their fears. An inventory of the hospital's supply of Pavulon — a synthetic version of Curare, the lethal plant toxin used by South American Indians to tip their poison darts — came up far short. Someone had methodically removed doses of the powerful drug from a locked room, the FBI concluded, and injected them into the intravenous medication systems of selected patients. Minutes after the Pavulon entered the victims' bloodstreams, their muscles, including diaphragms, were paralyzed.

The FBI launched an intense investigation to find out who had done it and why. Agents interviewed the hospital's staff, hypnotized patients who had survived the attacks, and exhumed the bodies of at least four of the dead victims. Ten months and a million dollars later, agents had narrowed the list of suspects to two nurses, Leonara Perez, 31, and Filipina Narciso, 29.

The two women, both Phillipine citizens, had been on duty when and where most of the incidents had occurred, during the afternoon shift in the intensive care unit. And several witnesses, including patients and their relatives, said that one or both of the nurses had been at many of the victims' bedsides minutes before they stopped breathing.

Still, Narciso and Perez seemed to be unlikely suspects. The two women had no prior criminal record or history of psychiatric instability. Each had lived and worked in the U.S. for only six years, and they had met each other for the first time only months before. To many observers it seemed ludicrous to believe that, for no apparent reason, the pair of nurses would plot together and carry out a bizarre plan to poison helpless patients under their care.

Nevertheless, on June 16, 1976, a grand jury indicted Perez and Narciso on charges of conspiracy, five counts of murder and 10 counts of poisoning. By the time their case came to trial nine months later, the prosecuting attorney inexplicably had dropped three of the murder charges and two of the poisoning charges.

The federal prosecutors called 78 witnesses, presented 40 exhibits — including the frozen organs of dead victims — and introduced thousands of pages of medical records. But after nine weeks, the government rested its case without establishing a motive or producing a single witness who had seen either Perez or Narciso inject Pavulon into any of the victims' intravenous tubes.

On June 8, 1977, the defense opened its case by submitting a motion to dismiss all charges for lack of evidence. The presiding judge did directly acquit Perez of two murders and four poisonings and Narciso of one murder and three poisonings. But Perez still faced charges for four poisonings and Narciso a murder and five poisonings.

In their opening remarks to the jury, defense attorneys portrayed the 10-floor, 430-bed VA hospital as being in near-continual chaos. The chronically understaffed facility was open to outsiders day and night, they said. Mental patients were often locked out of their rooms, forcing them to roam the hospital halls. Workers were not required to wear tags, badges or even uniforms, and visitors did not have to sign in and out. Security was so lax, concluded the defense, that just about anyone could have obtained and administered the Pavulon to the victims.

A former nursing supervisor at the VA hospital had, in fact, confessed to the killings while being treated at the University of Michigan's Neuropsychiatric Institute for, among other symptoms, acute guilt feelings. So reported the *Detroit Free Press*, citing as a source a man who was one of the patient's care-workers. The woman committed suicide before the trial, however, and defense attorneys could not get her records released because of doctor-patient privilege of confidentiality.

Another potential suspect was a man dressed in a green operating-room uniform. One of the patients Perez and Narciso were charged with poisoning testified that such a person had hovered over him just before he suffered a breathing failure. Another patient said that someone wearing green "pajamas" had entered his room and tampered with his roommate's intravenous tubes then fled shortly before the roommate suffered respiratory arrest and died. Several others testified they also saw a man in a green scrub suit near other patients who suffered breathing failures. But no one then or since has been able to identify the mysterious figure.

The defense rested after raising what appeared to be enormous reasonable doubt in the face of the prosecution's totally circumstantial evidence. Nevertheless, on July 13, 1977, after deliberating for 94 hours over 15 days, the jury of nine women and three men convicted Perez and Narciso of five nonfatal poisonings and a single count of conspiracy, but acquitted them of all other charges.

The convictions triggered demonstrations and protests by members of the medical profession, women's groups, the Phillipine government and others. During one rally 800 people — including uniformed nurses, pajama-clad patients, one of the jury alternates, and six Ypsilanti city councilmen — paraded around the VA hospital grounds, claiming that Perez and Narciso had been framed.

Defense attorneys, too, had complained before and during the trial that government attorneys were stacking the deck in their favor by not releasing, as required, evidence harmful to the prosecution's case. Transcripts of FBI interviews, for instance, were edited and some portions deleted. As a result Perez and Narciso had not received a fair trial, they argued.

The presiding judge agreed. In a 58-page opinion, he accused federal prosecutors of flagrant, unforgivable conduct and concluded that he was "left with the abiding conviction that this jury's verdicts could not reasonably have been reached free of the influence of the numerous improprieties . . . ." In December 1977 he overruled the jury's verdict and ordered a new trial.

On February 1, 1978, more than a year and a half after the original barrage of indictments against Perez and Narciso, the U.S. Attorney in charge of the case decided not to retry the nurses and dropped all remaining charges. No charges were ever filed against anyone else, and there have been no more unusual breathing failures at the VA Hospital.

ARE MICHIGAN HUNTERS THE PREY?

Is an unknown assailant stalking and killing sportsmen in remote areas of southwest Michigan, eastern Ohio and northeast Indiana? Law enforcement officials in those states and the FBI are seriously investigating the possibility. They say that the shooting deaths of at least eight outdoorsmen in recent years were not accidents and may be murders committed by the same killer.

Currently being investigated are the following incidents.

— Between April 1989 and April 1992, five men — two hunters, two fishermen and a hiker — were shot and killed in five different rural Ohio counties.

— On November 17, 1990, two Michigan hunters were shot to death in the Fulton State Game Area in Kalamazoo County. Though the victims did not know each other and were hunting separately, their bodies were found not far apart. Their own guns, which hadn't been fired, were lying nearby.

— One year later almost exactly to the day and only 80 miles away, a young man was slain while hunting on a family farm in northern Steuben County, Indiana.

Law enforcement officials have released few details except to say that the eight killings are suspiciously similar. Each of the two Michigan men were killed by a single 12-gauge shotgun blast in the back from close range. Other victims were shot sniper style from long distance with a high-powered rifle. All were killed while walking alone in remote areas.

With little other hard evidence or information to go on, investigators face frustrating questions. How does the killer pick his victims? What prompts him to strike? Is there a reason for choosing the victims, the time and the place? Why does the assailant jump across state lines?

To date there are no answers. "This guy, it's like he comes out of nowhere, kills for no reason, and disappears again," says one Kalamazoo County Sheriff's Department detective.

Investigators do agree on one frightening probability. The killer is a male who dresses like a hunter and looks no different than thousands of others who walk through the woods with loaded guns. They fear more outdoorsmen could die before he is discovered.

SUSPECTS AT THE SAULT

John Tanner and James Schoolcraft lived in vastly different worlds. Tanner, a white man raised by Indians, was forced into a life of poverty, squalor and misery. Schoolcraft, a member of one of early Michigan's most prominent families, enjoyed relative splendor. They knew of each other but probably never met. Yet both became tragically enmeshed in a murder that has puzzled investigators for nearly 150 years.

In August 1789, nine-year-old John Tanner left his family's log cabin in the Kentucky wilderness to fill his straw hat with walnuts from the surrounding forest. Moving through the same woods were two Shawnee Indians, a father and a son. When by chance they came upon young Tanner, they clapped a hand over his mouth and then took him by canoe and on foot to their settlement in the Saginaw Valley of Michigan. There the Indian father offered Tanner to his wife as a replacement for a young son who had recently died.

Tanner's Indian mother treated him kindly, but the men in his adoptive family and village starved, beat and overworked the young boy. After little more than a year, the Shawnee father became so disgusted by the sight of Tanner's pale face and deep-blue eyes, he cut the boy down with a tomahawk blow and left him for dead.

Tanner survived, but only to be purchased for 10 gallons of rum by the female chief of an Ottawa band from near present-day Petoskey. In 1800 Tanner and his Ottawa family moved to the Red River Country of Manitoba. Having been falsely told that his Kentucky family had been massacred, Tanner resigned himself to his fate and lived as an Indian for nearly 20 years. He excelled at hunting, fishing and other Indian skills. He spoke the Ottawa language fluently, married a young Indian woman, and raised a family.

Other Indians, however, never let him forget he was white. They verbally and physically abused Tanner, and even tried to kill him at least a half dozen times. Not surprisingly Tanner never abandoned the idea that he someday might return to white society. In 1819, at age 39, he finally made an attempt. Tanner moved his family to the Mackinac area, which had a reputation as a place where whites and Indians mixed well. There, he spent the next nine years sporadically working as an interpreter for the government, missionaries and fur trading companies.

But Tanner did not adapt well. He was unable or unwilling to transform himself back to being a white man, and he also would never be accepted by Indians. Tragically he was caught somewhere in between. Two wives — the first Indian, the second white — and several children all left him or were driven out. Consumed by frustration, Tanner grew increasingly withdrawn, mysterious and antisocial, often lashing out with violent verbal outbursts.

In 1828 Tanner's life looked like it might improve when he moved to Sault Ste. Marie to work as an interpreter for Henry Rowe Schoolcraft. Schoolcraft was well known throughout the territory and beyond as a scholar, author and Indian authority. His brother James was the chief provisioner to the army garrison at Ft. Brady. The Schoolcrafts were the "first family" of the Sault and often hosted gatherings of women in silk gowns and men in silver-buckled shoes and knee breeches.

But Tanner worked for Henry Schoolcraft only a few months, then was fired because, said Schoolcraft, he could no longer tolerate Tanner's rages. "(Tanner) is a gray-bearded, hard-featured old man whose feelings are at war with everyone on earth, white or red," Henry wrote in his journal.

Tanner, in turn, swore revenge.

Over the next 18 years, the "white Indian," as Tanner was called, became a total outcast. He lived alone in a small shack outside of town. His scowls, muttered threats and angry outbursts annoyed and frightened Sault Ste. Marie residents. Though there is no record of his ever being convicted, he was blamed for almost every unsolved crime that took place in the area.

Few were surprised, then, and most probably were relieved when, on the evening of July 4, 1846, John Tanner's shack burned to the ground and the white Indian disappeared. He evidently had left the area for good.

Any expectations of tranquility were shattered two days later. On July 6 James Schoolcraft took an afternoon walk down a path to a cleared field at the rear of his house. As he passed an area of thick undergrowth, a musket blasted a shot from less than four feet away. An ounce ball and three buckshot slammed into Schoolcraft's right side with such force it blew him cleanly out of the light slippers he wore. The ball pierced Schoolcraft's heart, and he fell dead on his face, the empty slippers marking his final steps.

Before Schoolcraft's body was removed from the scene, wanted posters naming Tanner as the murderer appeared throughout the village. Most people concluded that the white Indian had finally taken his revenge on Henry Rowe Schoolcraft by killing his brother. A reward was offered, and even Michigan Governor Alpheus Felch got involved, assuring Henry that he would do what he could to bring Tanner to trial.

A posse of army troops, woodsmen, Indians and yelping dogs, led by Lt. Bryant P. Tilden from Ft. Brady, spent weeks searching the surrounding woods and swamps for Tanner. They returned without finding any trace of him, and for the rest of the summer, Sault Ste. Marie area residents feared that Tanner still lurked in the area and would strike again.

However, not everyone then or now was convinced that Tanner had committed the murder. James Schoolcraft, it turns out, had made an enemy of his own. During a large Fourth of July party, Schoolcraft and Lt. Tilden had violently argued over the attentions of a woman. Several witnesses said they heard Tilden threaten to kill Schoolcraft. And, investigators determined, the fatal shot had been fired from an army musket.

Some thought that Tanner may have witnessed the murder. According to that speculation, while hiding in the area after he or someone else burned his cabin, Tanner by chance happened to see Tilden shoot Schoolcraft. Though Tilden probably wanted to then also kill Tanner, he couldn't because his single-shot gun was unloaded. And Tanner couldn't kill Tilden, because he certainly would have been charged with both murders. Tanner fled into the surrounding forest. Tilden returned to Ft. Brady, got himself placed in charge of the search party, and secured orders to shoot Tanner on sight. And some think that Tilden did catch and secretly slay Tanner.

Others believe that Tilden killed Tanner and burned his shack on July 4, then shot Schoolcraft two days later and blamed the murder on the "missing" white Indian.

Not long after the incident, Lt. Tilden and his garrison left to fight in the Mexican-American War. Tilden never returned to Michigan and died in Boston on December 27, 1859, at the age of 42. Rumors made their way back to Sault Ste. Marie that just before dying Tilden had admitted murdering James Schoolcraft. Whether the deathbed confession was true or not, it included no mention of what had happened to John Tanner.

Tanner's part in the murder and his fate will forever remain a mystery.

TINY WHITE COFFINS

On Christmas Eve 1913, in Calumet, Michigan, a mysterious man's shouts led to the mass deaths of more than 70 people. No one knows who he was or why he did it.

Whoever it was had been hurtling headlong with the rest of his Copper Country neighbors toward an almost inevitable disaster of some kind. The trouble began on July 22, 1913, when about 15,000 of the area's copper miners walked off their jobs, picketed all the major shafts in the Copper Country, and demanded unionization.

The strike quickly divided the community. Opponents organized into a group called the Citizens Alliance. They wore buttons denoting their allegiance and rallied behind the mining companies. Many other Copper Country residents, however, were sympathetic to the striking miners, most of whom were immigrants. Strikers and their supporters especially objected to the companies' policy of importing strikebreakers, including armed "thugs" from the slums of New York City, to work the mines.

The dispute soon turned violent and claimed victims on both sides. Striking miners physically attacked "scabs" who crossed picket lines, and company guards in turn beat the strikers. On August 14 a hail of bullets ripped through a boarding house and killed two striking miners. Almost four months later, three unidentified men fired 12 shots through the windows of another boarding house, where newly arrived strikebreaking workers were lodged. The bullets killed three men in their beds. That night Citizens Alliance members raided a union headquarters building and engaged in a brief but intense gun battle with the miners inside.

By mid-December the area had become an emotional powder keg. On December 24 someone lit the fuse.

Shortly after dark, hundreds of striking miners' children eagerly tramped through deep snow to Calumet's Italian Hall, where a women's auxiliary had organized a party. The women had obtained donated clothing, candy and other gifts from unions in large out-of-state cities, and had arranged for a local Santa to distribute them. The children, some accompanied by one or both parents, filed up a narrow stairway to the second floor, walked through a long cloakroom, and entered the hall. By the time the entertainment began, more than 600 people were jammed into the room.

Suddenly, as a woman played Christmas songs on the piano and Santa Claus distributed gifts, a large man wearing a hat and a long, dark overcoat with a fur collar turned up around his face yelled, "Fire! Fire!" The piano player leaped from the stage, ran toward the stranger and, while another woman reassured the uneasy children, told him to be quiet, that there was no fire. Then, in an effort to help calm the children, she ran back to the stage and began playing the piano again. As the man backed toward the doorway, he again shouted, "Fire! Fire!" and ran out.

A wave of panic-stricken children and adults swept after him through the doorway and jammed into the narrow corridor. As the children tripped and fell, they became stumbling blocks for others.

Within seconds, layers of bodies jammed the stairway. Double doors at the bottom of the stairwell opened outward, but the crush of people coming down wedged the bodies into an immovable wall a few feet from the exit. Those children who couldn't get through the jammed doorway ran around the hall room like terrified animals. Two crawled out a back window and fell to their deaths.

Someone pulled the fire alarm, and firemen raced from the station, only a block away. Jerking open the lower doors to the building, the chief reeled at the sight that greeted him. A pile of more than a hundred bodies, reaching halfway to the ceiling, squirmed a few feet from him.

While those at the bottom of the heap were dying of suffocation, firemen slammed ladders against the building, raced up to and through second-story windows, and began frantically pulling children off the top of the pile. Hands, legs and arms were so entangled that it took nearly an hour to sort through the pile of dead and moaning victims.

When the firemen finally finished their gruesome task, the bodies of 37 little girls, 19 small boys, 13 women and five men lay on the decorated tables in the hall.

Four days later, on the Sunday after Christmas, Calumet's churches conducted a mass funeral for the victims. At the conclusion of the services, with snow slowly falling, the fathers and brothers of the dead children picked up identical tiny white coffins and walked two miles over snow-covered roads to the cemetery.

Who had caused the deaths and why? Strike sympathizers blamed the Citizen's Alliance. Several survivors said that the man who had shouted the fatal call was wearing an Alliance button, although no one recognized or could identify him. Was he an Alliance member, perhaps intending only to disrupt a brief, happy moment in the lives of strikers? Or was the motive more sinister, perhaps deadly revenge for the killings of the four strikebreakers?

The man couldn't have been an Alliance member, defenders said, because anyone entering the Italian Hall that evening was required to show a union card to a doorkeeper at the lone entrance. But the mass of people crowding into the hall would have made it easy for someone to sneak by without a card. Or for that matter, a union card probably would not have been too difficult to come by.

Could a striking miner have been the culprit? Perhaps someone who only intended to cause disruption not death and set it up to look like the work of the Alliance to create sympathy for the strikers? Was a drunk's impaired attempt at a practical joke to blame? Directly below the hall was a saloon frequented by strikers.

With the community torn asunder, it was impossible to find out.

The following April the strike officially ended. But one by one in the ensuing years, the depleted copper mines shut down. And by droves, most everyone who had been caught up in the bitter, tragic labor dispute — including, quite likely, the man responsible for the bodies in the tiny white coffins — left the area for good.

MISSING PERSONS

Each year thousands of Michigan residents are reported missing. Most are runaways — teenagers upset with their home or school life or adults trying to escape unhappy marriages, family pressures, legal problems or financial setbacks. Some missing persons are murder victims whose bodies have been destroyed or hidden. No matter the reason, eventually almost everyone who disappears is found, returns, or is otherwise accounted for.

In a few puzzling and frightening instances, however, ordinary people going about their ordinary lives have inexplicably vanished.

Following are two such recent cases.

GONE HUNTING

On November 22, 1985, David Tyll and Brian Ognjan threw guns and gear into Tyll's Ford Bronco, cashed a check, and then headed north out of Metro Detroit for a Thanksgiving weekend of deer hunting. Somewhere en route they and their vehicle vanished.

The ongoing search for the pair has turned up more unanswered questions than clues, and their strange disappearance remains one of Michigan's most-puzzling unsolved mysteries.

Tyll, 27, of Troy, and Ognjan, 28, of St. Clair Shores, had arranged their trip well in advance. The two, friends since their Boy Scout days together, were headed to Tyll's family's cabin near White Cloud in Newaygo County. Relatives in town and hunting buddies at the cabin were awaiting them. On the morning of November 23, Tyll's wife and Ognjan's parents received phone calls from White Cloud wondering why the two men hadn't arrived.

Their families hadn't heard from them either, and so they notified authorities. Police searched the area near the White Cloud cabin as well as two other hunting camps, in eastern Roscommon County, where the two men might have gone. There were no signs that Tyll and Ognjan had come anywhere near those places.

Tyll's wife and Ognjan's fiancee rented a helicopter to fly over the dense Manistee Forest around White Cloud, hoping for a glimpse of Tyll's shiny, black 1980 Bronco. The aerial search, too, revealed nothing, but the missing hunters' families were heartened by the report of a psychic who reported that both men "were around."

Media coverage was extensive, and few Michigan residents missed seeing photos of Tyll and Ognjan on television or in newspapers. The men's families also distributed more than 1,000 flyers bearing the missing hunters' pictures and physical descriptions to shopping malls, convenience stores, physician's offices, gas stations — anywhere they could get them posted — throughout Michigan and beyond. The barrage of publicity also hit the hundreds of up-north bars where hunters congregate.

At one a waitress said she remembered serving two men, one of whom she thought might have been Ognjan. State Police officers interviewed the woman, and the identification seemed to check out.

Investigators and the missing men's families were encouraged by the breakthrough, but they were also stunned by a totally unexpected development. The bar where Ognjan was spotted was nowhere near the men's planned route. It was in Mio, more than 100 miles northeast of White Cloud.

Police then traced Tyll and Ognjan to a second Mio-area bar and then a third, where they were last seen about 9 p.m. on November 24. A shirt believed to be worn by Tyll was left on one of the bar stools. Police are certain that Tyll and Ognjan were in Mio. But to this day, no one has any idea why the two men decided to drive to an area unfamiliar to them (one witness said men matching their description had asked for directions to Grayling, a few miles west of Mio). And why hadn't the otherwise dependable pair notified their families or hunting buddies at White Cloud of their change in plans.

Extensive air and ground searches of the Mio-Grayling area turned up no further evidence of the fate or whereabouts of the men or their black Bronco. And in the years since, police have been frustrated by the continued lack of solid leads. A couple of what appeared to be reliable tips led to searches of the backwaters of two dams. In 1989 police divers probed Loud Dam Pond in Iosco County. And in May 1991 eight divers, using special metal-detecting gear rented from the University of Michigan by Tyll's and Ognjan's parents, spent three days scouring the bottom at Alcona Dam Pond in Alcona County. The searches turned up no traces of vehicle parts or bodies.

Based on recent evidence, police now think that Tyll and Ognjan may have spent their last hours in yet a fourth bar, one near South Branch. There, police believe, an altercation that began inside may have ended shortly after closing time when Tyll and Ognjan were jumped by a group of men who were waiting in the parking lot. Police say they even have suspects — three brothers and a friend — but no hard evidence or witnesses.

Police hope that the $15,000 reward put up by the missing men's families and advertised on posters around the Mio-Curtisville-South Branch area will prompt someone to come forward with new information. Or maybe one of the thousands of hunters who flock to the area each fall might stumble across a fresh clue or overhear a loose word. Perhaps then it will become clear how and why David Tyll and Brian Ognjan vanished into the north woods.

THE MISSING MOTORIST

On May 24, 1990, in full view of midafternoon traffic, 30-year-old Paige Renkoski pulled her car to a stop on the shoulder of I-96, stepped out and vanished. Police still have little idea how.

Earlier that Thursday morning, Renkoski had driven her mother from their home in Okemos to Detroit Metro Airport. After seeing her mother off, Renkoski, a nursery school teacher, drove the family's 1986 silver Oldsmobile Cutlass Calais to a girlfriend's house in Canton Township, in western Wayne County. The pair went to nearby Griffin Park, where they visited for several hours while watching the friend's two children play. At about 2:30 p.m., Renkoski made her way onto I-96 and then headed west back to Okemos, near Lansing.

She didn't make it. At about 3:30, a passing motorist noticed — but thought little of it — the silver Cutlass, its lights on, stopped on the shoulder about a half mile east of the Fowlerville exit, in Livingston County. When the same motorist passed by again nearly five hours later and saw the car still there, with its lights still on, he called police. Livingston County Sheriff's Department officers arrived and found that the Oldsmobile's engine was still running. The doors were unlocked, and inside they found Renkoski's shoes and her purse containing money and I.D. There were no skid marks, no damage to the vehicle, no evidence of a struggle, and no sign of the driver.

Police called in a helicopter and nine tracking dogs and searched a 500-acre wooded area near the freeway. They found no trace of Paige Renkoski nor any clues as to what might have happened to her. Over the next several months, a 20-person police task force sifted through tips that flooded in as a result of heavy media coverage, including two national network crime shows.

Renkoski's family — mother, father and two sisters — were also active in the investigation. They distributed nearly 30,000 yellow missing-person circulars throughout southeast Michigan. And using space and ads donated by several companies, they placed 10- x 10-foot pictures of Paige Renkoski on 25 billboards in high-traffic areas throughout southern Michigan and northern Ohio. The family even hired a psychic, who turned over a four-page report to investigating officers.

The enormous efforts by police and family members produced a single vague, frustrating clue. Ten passers-by said that, at about 3 p.m., they had seen a woman fitting Renkoski's description — blond hair, blue eyes, 5-feet-7-inches tall, 125 pounds — talking to a man while standing on the shoulder between her car and a maroon minivan. At least two of the 10 witnesses were hypnotized to see if they could come up with more information, such as a license plate number, but they remembered nothing further.

Police knew about the man and the van less than a week after Renkoski's disappearance, but they have uncovered scant new evidence since. Investigators received more than 700 tips in the year following the disappearance, but leads then dwindled to next to none.

Filling the void are theories, speculations and unanswered questions.

Some experts think Renkoski may have been the victim — perhaps not the first — of a serial sexual killer who may have followed her from Metro Airport or Griffin Park. Several murder or missing persons cases in the months before and after Renkoski's disappearance were also linked to one of those areas.

"We've looked for a connection," a crime analyst with the Detroit FBI Office was quoted as saying. "But to do that, you have to have something where you can determine a pattern. And when you have a disappearance, you don't have anything." In the absence of evidence, the question of whether or not a serial killer is involved remains open.

Renkoski's family wonders how *anyone* could have persuaded her to pull off the freeway, stop, and get out of her car. She didn't have car trouble; the Oldsmobile's engine was still running hours after she had disappeared. There was no evidence her vehicle was forced off the road. Was the man in the maroon minivan someone she knew or perhaps had met even that day? Was he a stranger posing as a law enforcement officer?

Investigators say they are no closer to answering those and other questions than the day Paige Renkoski vanished. Says one official, "All we know is that it's pretty unlikely (she) left on her own."

GREAT LAKES
MYSTERIES

The Great Lakes make up the largest body of fresh water in the world. Together they cover almost 100,000 square miles and are rightly called North America's "inland seas."

And these freshwater seas can be every bit as treacherous as the world's salt-water oceans. Though the Great Lakes are vast, they are relatively shallow. They vary in average depth from 200 to 600 feet, with only Lake Superior plunging to occasional depths of 1,300 feet. As a result, strong winds can quickly turn flat, calm surfaces into violent, moving mountains of water. During the past three centuries, deadly Great Lakes storms have claimed tens of thousands of lives.

Weather isn't the only reason thousands of ships and hundreds of aircraft traversing the lakes have not made it to their destinations. Collisions, equipment failures, human error, and a variety of other causes have also sent craft, crews and passengers to their deaths. The list of casualties and their causes is so horribly long and varied that some even claim there must be more than just natural forces at work. The Great Lakes, they say, have a mysterious destructive power of unknown or alien origin that rivals that of the infamous Bermuda Triangle.

But after almost all accidents, there's enough evidence to determine in conventional ways what happened, when, where and often why. Most tragedies are explainable, understandable and, in some instances, predictable.

There have been, however, a few strange happenings on the lakes that defy easy or sometimes *any* explanation. Following are five such mysteries that took place in Michigan Great Lakes waters.

IMPOSSIBLE ENCOUNTER

It wasn't surprising that, in the aftermath of one of the most violent storms ever recorded, stranded ships, wreckage and bodies littered the Great Lakes shorelines. But the peculiar condition of some of Lake Huron's victims turned what should have been a clearly explainable tragedy into one of the Great Lakes greatest mysteries.

The storm formed over the western end of Lake Superior on November 6, 1913, and grew stronger as it moved southeast. Three days later, gale warning flags flew over nearly all Great Lakes ports, but they didn't stop many ships from casting off and joining several dozen already on the open water. November trips — the all-important last few runs of the shipping season — were always rough. Most crews, their sturdy ships, and experienced pilots had ridden them out many times before.

As was typical the winds were out of the northwest, so the captains of vessels headed up or down Lake Huron were less concerned than others. They could set a course that hugged the Michigan shoreline and put them on the lee side of the weather.

That was the plan of the captain of the *Charles S. Price* as he eased his 524-foot-long steamer—carrying 28 crew members and 9,000 tons of soft coal—up the St. Clair River past Port Huron at 6 a.m., Sunday, November 9th. Across the river at Sarnia, Ontario, the 250-foot-long package freighter *Regina* was taking on a cargo that included eight rail cars of canned goods and 140 tons of baled hay. At about noon the *Regina* and its 25-man crew pulled away from the docks and also headed out into Lake Huron and a fate shared by dozens of other ships and hundreds of sailors on all five Great Lakes that day.

By late afternoon the worst storm ever to hit America's "inland seas" was peaking. Winds roared at near-hurricane force, and waves to 35 feet crashed into steel hulls, twisting and bending them until rows of rivets popped like a firing machine gun. As the temperature plummeted, the walls of water added layer upon heavy layer of ice to decks. And the wind-driven snow was so thick that men in pilot houses couldn't see the bows of their ships.

When the storm finally eased the next day, 11 vessels had sunk and another 30 were severely damaged. Two hundred thirty-five sailors had lost their lives.

Uncharacteristically, Lake Huron ships had taken the brunt of the fury. Freak weather conditions had suddenly shifted winds to the northeast, from which they howled at 60-70 mph for over 12 hours. Caught in the teeth of the storm, eight modern steel freighters went to the bottom of Lake Huron with not a single survivor. Among the victims were the *Regina*, the *Price* and their crews.

After the storm, prevailing westerly winds washed bodies, cargo and wreckage from Lake Huron onto the Canadian shore. For a week, farm wagons carried the dead from remote Ontario beaches through deep snow to makeshift morgues in little coastal towns.

During the grim process of identifying the victims, a coroner at Thedford (30 miles north of Sarnia) recorded a puzzling observation. A dozen bodies positively identified as being from the crew of the *Price* were wearing life preservers marked *"Regina."*

This eerie discovery, which quickly made national headlines, defied logical explanation. The last reported sightings of the two up-bound ships — apparently not long before they went down — placed them more than 15 miles and several hours apart. The condition of bodies and other evidence also suggested that the *Price* had sunk suddenly and unexpectedly. How then had some of the *Price* crew managed to strap on *Regina* lifejackets in their desperate attempt to survive? After more than 80 years, there still is no conclusive answer.

Initially, the explanation seemed obvious. In the fierce storm, one or both ships must have changed or been blown off course, and in the near-zero visibility the two had slammed together. In the confusion following the collision, men may have been able to jump from one ship deck to another and grab any available life jacket. Also, the jackets could have been tossed back and forth between the ships or to crew members who had been knocked into the water. It sounded plausible for a short time, until it was announced that not a single body from the *Regina*'s crew was wrapped in a *Price* lifejacket.

Some then speculated that after the collision the crippled vessels were together so briefly a dozen of the *Price*'s crew were the only ones who had time to switch ships. When the *Regina* later began sinking, the *Price* men aboard strapped on and ultimately died in the *Regina*'s life jackets.

That theory held water for a week, until a capsized "mystery ship" that had floated into Port Huron the day after the storm was finally identified. It was the *Price*, and it showed no evidence of having been involved in a collision.

The *Regina* wasn't found until nearly 73 years later. When scuba divers finally discovered and examined its remains — in July 1986 off Pt. Sanilac, Michigan—they reported that the *Regina*, too, showed no markings or signs of a collision.

How else then in the midst of what some have called a "freshwater hurricane" could the 12 *Price* men have come to die in *Regina* lifejackets? Some theories are beyond the reach of the long arm of coincidence. Author Frederick Stonehouse, for instance, in his book *Went Missing*, speculates that the *Regina* happened to catch up to the *Price* immediately before or after the *Price* capsized. In the few moments before the storm again separated the two vessels, the *Regina* crew, Stonehouse says, managed to get one of their ship's lifeboats, containing lifejackets, over to the *Price*. The *Price* crew members who scrambled into the boat and put on the jackets, however, were quickly overcome by the monstrous waves and drowned. But Stonehouse concedes that — considering the vast water that had originally separated the ships, the near-zero visibility, and fluke timing required — such a chance encounter was less than remote.

Paul J. Schmitt, a professor at St. Clair Community College, reversed Stonehouse's theory after thoroughly studying photographs and data obtained from the wreck of the *Regina*. It might have been the *Price*, he said in a 1987 *Inland Seas* magazine article, that happened to come across *Regina* survivors. The *Price*, Schmitt thinks, may have turned south and made a run back for the shelter of the St. Clair River. In doing so its course took it through the wreckage from the *Regina*, which had already sunk. *Regina* survivors in lifeboats signaled to the *Price*, and when the *Price* captain turned his ship to help, the huge, cumbersome freighter got caught in a trough between the waves and capsized. The *Regina* survivors then threw their extra lifejackets to the *Price* crew members who had been thrown into the icy water.

But, Schmitt admits, there's really no way to prove his theory. It's a secret, he says, known only to Lake Huron.

THE TREASURE OF POVERTY ISLAND

Is there $200 million in gold coins resting on the bottom of Lake Michigan, conveniently packaged in five chests chained together, just waiting for some lucky or persistent diver to find them? For 130 years stories that have circulated among sailors and treasure hunters and in newspapers, magazines and lakeside taverns say there is.

According to the mother of all the tales, during the American Civil War, French Emporer Napoleon III wanted to secretly aid the South. So during the late summer of 1863, Napoleon's agents transported $5 million in French gold coins through Canada to Escanaba, Michigan. There the money, sealed in five steel-banded chests, was loaded onto a brigantine that was to be sailed down Lake Michigan to Chicago. From Chicago the secret funds were to be transported to the Mississippi River and then south to Confederate leaders.

A sea captain working as a war smuggler set sail with the gold. Unknown to the ship's crew, French-Canadian pirates, who had found out about the gold cargo from a spy, set out after them. The pirates overtook the treasure ship near Poverty Island, about 27 miles southeast of Escanaba. As the brig was being fired upon, the captain ordered the five chests chained together and, out of the sight of the pirates, thrown overboard. If he couldn't flee and his ship were captured, reasoned the brig's captain, the pirates would let them go after finding no gold. The brig and its crew could then return later and salvage the submerged contraband. But when the pirates caught up to the brig and found no gold aboard, they killed the captain and crew and sunk the ship.

The legends say the chests still lie somewhere beneath the waves that lap the shores of tiny, remote Poverty Island. And because the water there is deep and cold, the treasure, now worth close to $200 million, should be perfectly preserved.

Some Great Lakes historians and experts have dismissed the story as pure fiction, unsubstantiated by facts or evidence. Others, however, have said it's not surprising there's no documentation. Napoleon's operation, after all, was clandestine, and pirates certainly don't keep ships logs. The chests and their contents are there, somewhere, they say.

In fact the treasure was once almost recovered, according to another well-circulated story. During the late 1920s, a rescue vessel was attempting to free a freighter stranded on the rocky shoals that surround Poverty Island by lowering anchors and winching on them. One anchor snagged a length of chain and pulled some chests close to the surface where they were visible for a few seconds before sinking again. Details of the incident, supposedly told by the crews of both ships, circulated throughout Great Lakes ports.

When the reports reached Chicago a few years later, one group became so excited that, according to a March 1969 article in *Skin Diver* magazine, they raised $35,000 during the Depression to fund a hunt for the treasure. Nearly every day for three consecutive summers, a team of divers headed by Frank Pea went beneath the waves in a diving bell lowered from the ship *St. Lawrence*. According to the same article, the curious young son of a Poverty Island lighthouse keeper watched the salvage operation with interest. Upon reaching middle age, he began telling people that when the diving bell came up one day late during the third summer he could clearly hear excited shouts and laughter from the men aboard. The boy concluded they had located the gold.

But before they could retrieve the chests, a terrible storm wiped out the diving bell and the *St. Lawrence*. The fortune hunters were also wiped out of funds and never returned.

Some doubt they were ever there. The lighthouse keeper's son is real, but there are no official records anywhere of a ship named *St. Lawrence* or of a Captain Frank Pea.

That hasn't deterred the enthusiasm of countless divers who have spent varying portions of their lives and assets trying to find the elusive gold coins. Psychics, faith healers and dowsers have shown up, too, certain they knew where the chests were. A computer expert once even attempted to locate the treasure by digitally enhancing satellite photos of the area.

Probably the most serious searcher is Richard Bennett, a professional diver and diving instructor from the Milwaukee, Wisconsin area. Just about every summer since 1967, 54-year-old Bennett has painstakingly combed sections of the roughly 2-square-mile area of hard-clay and clean-rock Lake Michigan bottom where he has calculated the treasure lies. In 1985 at a cost of $25,000, he even built a 14-foot submarine, complete with its own water heater to keep him and his fellow divers warm.

To date, however, all Bennett and the others have discovered is where the $200 million jackpot isn't. No one can say for sure, yet, that the gold-filled chests exist. All that's certain is that others will continue the search for the five speculative specks on Lake Michigan's bottom.

THE UNKNOWN FATE OF FLIGHT 2501

One of the most mysterious disasters in U.S. aviation history took place over South Haven, Michigan, on June 23, 1950. Shortly before midnight a four-engine, 20-ton DC-4 carrying 58 people suddenly vanished from the sky. The fate of the plane and its occupants has never been determined.

The flight started out no differently than the dozens of others out of New York's La Guardia airport that night. Passengers taking advantage of Northwest Airlines special night rates began boarding the high-tailed "air coach" shortly before 8 p.m. EST. Most were vacationers, including families, headed to Minneapolis, the scheduled first stop, or Seattle, at the end of the line. Some were college students returning home from Eastern institutions. A Roman Catholic priest, who rushed aboard at the last minute, filled the plane to its 55-passenger capacity.

At 8:25, 35-year-old Capt. Robert C. Lind and his co-pilot, Verne Wolfe, lifted flight 2501 into the warm, humid air. Stewardess Bonnie Feldman moved through the passenger section as the DC-4 passed uneventfully over Lake Erie and then the lights of Detroit. At

10:52 Capt. Lind radioed that he was on course above Battle Creek.

Twenty-one minutes later he made another routine broadcast. He was crossing the shoreline near South Haven, he told the ground station, and could see lightning lashing the area ahead of him out over Lake Michigan. Because of the storm, he asked permission to descend a thousand feet from his assigned 3,500-foot altitude. Air-traffic controllers, however, denied his request because there were too many planes already assigned to the lower altitude.

Lind headed the DC-4 across Lake Michigan anyway. His next scheduled radio check-in was to be with the Milwaukee ground station, about 25 minutes later. The plane was never heard from again.

By sunrise on June 24, one of the most extensive searches in the history of Lake Michigan was in full operation. The Coast Guard, Navy, Air Force, Civil Aviation Administration, Civil Air Patrol, local police forces and Northwest Airlines sent out hundreds of aircraft and boats.

The planes and ships criss-crossed Lake Michigan along the general path the DC-4 should have taken. Had Northwest 2501 suddenly exploded in flight, as was likely because there was no distress call, the searchers were sure to find Lake Michigan littered with floating wreckage. If mechanical trouble, lightning, or some other problem had caused the plane to crash into the water, the 2,500 gallons of fuel it was carrying would paint the surface with a multicolor slick. The entire hull, four sturdy engines, or other large portions of the craft should remain intact to either sink to the bottom or possibly still be floating on the surface. There might even be survivors.

But even helped by ideal conditions — sunny, clear skies and calm waters — the rescue armada found no evidence of a crash. A few large oil slicks turned out to be from the bilge water of Great Lakes ships. Off shore from Milwaukee, the crew of a destroyer escort spotted pieces of paper and oil bubbling up. A diver made three descents to the bottom 66 feet below but found only rocks. Other ships picked up isolated pieces of floating debris, but none was from Northwest Flight 2501. And there were no signs that the plane had crashed on land in either Michigan or Wisconsin.

Toward the end of the second day, the Coast Guard finally came across some remains of Flight 2501. Floating on the surface about 10 miles due west of South Haven was the aircraft's log book.

Nearby were a couple of scraps of clothing and a piece of blue blanket marked with the initials, N.W. Bobbing just under the surface were what appeared to be a few small pieces of human flesh.

Confident that the wreckage of the DC-4 was lying at the bottom, the Coast Guard sent down divers. They scoured the area but found nothing. Navy antisubmarine experts then swept a huge section of the lake with sophisticated sonar and radar devices. They, too, failed to detect any submerged metallic objects. Inexplicably, the huge plane and 58 human bodies had somehow almost completely disintegrated or disappeared.

On June 29, 1950, the search was called off, and the Civil Aeronautics Board (CAB) began their official inquiry into what, at the time, was the worst commercial aviation disaster in U.S. history. They interviewed air-traffic controllers. They investigated the backgrounds of Flight 2501's crew and thoroughly examined the history of the plane itself. But the next year, they too gave up, stating in their official report that there simply wasn't enough evidence to determine what had happened or why.

Flight 2501 had officially flown into oblivion.

DOUBLE DISAPPEARANCE

The hundreds of shipwrecks that have taken place in Michigan's Great Lakes waters, though often dramatic, have not been particularly mysterious. Wreckage and bodies that eventually float to the surface, wash ashore or are discovered by divers, usually give clues as to what caused the destruction, when and where.

One double tragedy, however, has defied explanation for more than 75 years. In 1918 two ships and their crews, traveling together across Lake Superior, literally vanished without a trace. To many, the fate of the missing ships is the most puzzling mystery in Great Lakes sailing history.

The disappearance of the *Inkerman* and the *Cerisoles*, was not only mysterious, but also surprising. The pair were part of a fleet of 12 identical vessels, all built to withstand not only the worst Great Lakes sailing conditions, but also a potentially wilder Atlantic Ocean crossing. The sturdy, compact 143-foot steel minesweepers were constructed at a

Ft. William, Ontario, shipyard for the French government, which planned to muster them into World War I duty in European harbors. (After the war one of the ships was used to break through heavy Arctic ice on the famed 1924 Byrd-MacMillan Expedition.)

On Saturday morning, November 23, 1918, three of the mine-sweepers — the *Inkerman*, *Cerisoles* and *Sebastapol* — set sail from Thunder Bay together, bound for the Soo Locks and eventually France. Each was manned by 38 sailors of the French navy. Each was radio-equipped and had an experienced Canadian Great Lakes pilot aboard. French Naval Captain Leclerc was in charge and took the lead in the *Sebastapol*.

The next day, visibility gradually diminished, and during the night heavy weather, including thick snow, swept the eastern area of the lake. Winds howled from the southwest, so Captain Leclerc ordered his small fleet to sail into the blast toward the Keweenaw Peninsula. There they were to make a turn to the northeast and, in the shelter of land, sail around Keweenaw Point and then on to Whitefish Point.

During the maneuver the *Sebastapol* lost sight of and radio contact with the *Inkerman* and *Cerisoles*. Confident that the two ships were not far behind, Leclerc continued on, reaching the Soo on November 26.

Several days later the *Inkerman* and *Cerisoles* still hadn't arrived. Fearing the worst, Leclerc chartered a tug and combed hundreds of miles of the Canadian Lake Superior shore looking for wreckage. Meanwhile, the U.S. Coast Guard swept the American mainland shore plus the Isle Royale area. Passing lake freighters were asked by radio if they had seen any evidence of the missing vessels.

But not a scrap of wreckage, no bodies, and no clues have ever been found. The two new minesweepers and their officers, crew and Canadian pilots simply vanished from the lake.

Whatever happened occurred so fast that neither ship had time to radio a distress call or launch lifeboats. Yet whatever happened was not violent enough to create any wreckage. Somehow, for reasons no one has been able to determine, Lake Superior somehow swallowed the ships and crew whole, in one quick gulp. Or, as 19th century sailors used to say about lost ships, it was as though the *Inkerman* and *Cerisoles* had sailed into a crack in the lake.

VERSHWINDEN

Throughout more than 300 years of Great Lakes sailing tragedies, countless captains — as nautical decorum dictates — have gone down with their ships. But in one strange modern-day incident, a skipper evidently went down without his ship, and no one knows how or why.

In late October 1987, the 579-foot freighter *Serius*, sailing under the flag of the Grand Cayman Islands, dropped off a load of steel in Chicago and then headed up Lake Michigan toward the Soo Locks and eventually Duluth, Minnesota, where it would take on a cargo of grain. Shortly before 2 a.m. on October 21, Captain Frederich Helling surveyed the calm seas and set a course that would take his ship between Ludington and South Fox Island. The stout 48-year-old West German then retired for the night to his cabin at the ship's stern. He was scheduled to report back on deck at 8 a.m.

The normally punctual captain, however, didn't show, and crew members immediately conducted a ship-wide search. At 11 a.m., failing to turn up any sign of Helling, they radioed the Coast Guard for assistance. Helling, they reported, had disappeared, evidently into the 53-degree F. waters.

Within minutes the Coast Guard sent a helicopter and three 44-foot boats to the region where the captain had presumably gone overboard. Retracing the course the *Serius* had taken during the night, the Coast Guard craft scoured a 900-square mile area of Lake Michigan. Several days later they called off the search and put out an alert to all ships traveling the lake to be on the lookout for Helling's body.

Meanwhile, an investigation had also been launched on shore. Because U.S. law allows federal jurisdiction over crimes committed in U.S. waters, the Detroit office of the FBI and U.S. Attorney John Smietanka, in Grand Rapids, conducted the inquiry into what had happened to Frederich Helling.

They set out to prove one of three possible theories: suicide, accident or murder. However, there was virtually no physical evidence, only a few pieces of clothing that seemed to be missing from Helling's quarters. Their only hope was that someone on the ship had seen or heard something. The Coast Guard detained the *Serius* at

Sault Ste. Marie, where FBI agents interrogated a third of the 35-man crew. The rest were questioned two days later while the ship was anchored at Duluth.

Though a few crew members said Helling seemed to suffer abrupt mood swings, investigators concluded that the captain was not a classic candidate for suicide. Helling's friends described him as up-beat and happily married. There was no suicide note, and in his last letter to his wife, Helling wrote that he was very much looking forward to spending time with her and their two teen-age children.

An accident also seemed unlikely. The weather had been fair and seas calm, so Helling certainly hadn't been washed overboard. He was not known to drink much and had no history of fainting or blackouts. Besides, a 3 1/2-foot safety railing that completely sur-rounded the ship would have made it almost impossible for the 5-foot-8-inch-tall captain to fall overboard under any conditions.

Perhaps, speculated some seamen, Helling may have deliberately gone past the railing on his own and then accidentally plunged into the water. The *Serius'* lifeboats, they pointed out, are suspended above the deck just outside the captain's cabin. The protective railing passes underneath the life rafts, and about three more feet of deck extends past the railing. Helling, they said, might have heard a noise, gone out to check, and discovered that a lifeboat was loose. He then may have climbed over the railing to secure it and slipped overboard.

Such an act, however, would have violated shipboard procedures that required Helling to be secured and watched by another seaman. Helling's shipping company superiors and crew members all agreed that the 30-year veteran sailor was much too careful, smart and expe-rienced to have pulled such a reckless stunt. The only way their captain would have gone over the rail, they said, was if someone lifted or pushed him.

U.S. Attorney Smietanka, for reasons he never revealed, was con-vinced that was exactly what had happened, that Helling had been murdered. But from all reports, the popular captain was well liked by everyone aboard the *Serius*. The FBI's exhaustive interviews with all 35 crew members did not reveal a single finger-pointing clue.

Whatever had happened to Helling, just about everyone agreed that his body would eventually wash up somewhere on the Michigan shoreline. A subsequent autopsy might then shed some light on the mystery. A body, however, was never recovered.

Somehow, Capt. Frederich Helling had, as his German countrymen would say, *vershwinden* — vanished.

HISTORIC AND PREHISTORIC MYSTERIES

To most of us, the study of Michigan history appears to be straightforward and linear — basically a string of dates attached to events that help portray life in Michigan's past. By methodically digging up artificats and plodding through old journals, records and diaries, historians continue to fill in missing gaps and add details. What they uncover or discover usually fits neatly into the tidy, orderly sequence.

But not always. Historians, too, have come across their share of curious, occasionally dramatic anomolies.

MYSTERIOUS MESSAGES FROM THE PAST

Jutting out from sandy loam above the Cass River near New Greenleaf is the most mysterious chunk of rock in Michigan. Scratched into the 15- by 40-foot sandstone outcropping are at least 100 rare and puzzling markings that include depictions of strange creatures, animal tracks, abstract patterns and human figures.

What the carvings are is no mystery. They are petroglyphs, that is works of art painstakingly hammered, gouged, scratched and chiseled into the soft rock by prehistoric Native Americans using bones, antlers, sharp stones and other simple tools. But *who* did the carvings, *when*, and perhaps most importantly, *why*, are questions that may never be satisfactorily answered.

That's not because nobody's tried. These Sanilac Petroglyphs, as they've been named, are the only known Indian rock carvings in Michigan. As such, they've been thoroughly examined by hundreds of professionals and amateurs since forest fires exposed the intriguing slab of sandstone in the 1880s. Researchers from both Michigan State University and the Michigan Department of State, for instance, have tried to determine the carvings' age by using carbon dating, links to artifacts found in the area, and other standard archaeological methods.

So far, however, they have not been able to say for certain when ancient Michiganians may have created the petroglyphs. Most scientists agree that they were probably carved during what is called the Woodland Era, which makes them anywhere from 400 to 1,100 years old.

There's less agreement about who did the drawings and why. They're obviously more than just prehistoric doodles or graffiti. It's unlikely that any ancient Native American would spend hours or days hunched over the rock carefully scraping designs with crude tools just for fun. What important meaning did the figures have to the carver, or what special messages were they supposed to communicate to others? There are no certain answers, only fascinating speculation.

Many of the images depict what are obviously human figures, partial or full. Who do they represent? Some say gods, others believe ancestors, and a few think maybe the carver himself. The most-deeply carved, visible figure is a foot-tall likeness of a man wearing a triangle-shaped headdress, standing with his feet apart, and holding a bow drawn into a shooting position. A single continuous line forms his arm and arrow. Was this the boastful work of a macho young hunter or warrior? A sign to others that hunting was good here? Or perhaps an early "Private Hunting, No Trespassing" warning.

Many of the figures represent wildlife. Were the deer, fox, a long line of geese, and the rabbit and bear tracks etched as a record of a successful hunt? Or were they perhaps created during periodic pre-hunt rituals or ceremonies to produce magic or luck?

And where did the clearly imaginary creatures — including carvings of several beasts with long wrap-around tails — fit into the minds and myths of the culture that drew them?

Some of the line drawings themselves are perplexing. Not even the most dedicated glyph-examiners have deciphered what messages were intended by the spirals, crosses, waves, and other abstract patterns.

And finally, who created these remarkable glimpses into the lives of Michigan's prehistoric inhabitants — medicine men, chiefs, tribal historians? Or are they simply the expressions of aboriginal artists. All of the above?

We may never fully discover the answers, because the rare relic of Michigan's prehistory is rapidly deteriorating. Vandals have scratched their initials into the rock, and at least four of the carvings have been completely chiseled out and removed from the site. Michigan's harsh climate has taken a toll, too. The elements have completely erased some of the more-shallow carvings, and the rest are fading, grain by sandy grain. Today, the low outcropping is covered by a wood roof and is surrounded by a locked, gated chain-link fence on rural land designated but not developed as a state park.

Such measures protect but cannot preserve, and there may not be enough time left to learn the mysterious secrets of the extraordinary piece of rock art. Says John Halsey, State of Michigan Archaeologist, "The challenge offered by the Sanilac Petroglyphs to rational modern interpretation may endure until they have disappeared."

GROUNDS FOR QUESTION

When early explorers and settlers moved through the river valleys of southwestern Michigan, they occasionally came across some peculiar markings in the prairie sod. The elaborate patterns of ridges and furrows appeared to be manmade but with a level of skill and sophistication not attributable to any known Native American people who had ever lived in the region. To this day the origin, meaning and purpose of the ancient creations remain mysteries.

The rare discoveries consisted of symmetrical, 6- to 18-inch-high ridges of soil precisely laid out in a variety of carefully planned, near-perfect geometric patterns. Near present-day Kalamazoo, for instance, several dozen straight lines of raised ground radiated from a circular center ridge out to another circular ridge to form a 90-foot-in-diameter "wagon wheel." The largest configuration, a series of rectangles near present-day Three Rivers, covered nearly 120 acres. Other patterns — ranging from simple parallelograms to complex combinations of lines and curves — marked the ground at 20 more sites, most located in St. Joseph, Cass and Kalamazoo counties. In fact, except for a couple of possible locations in Indiana and Wisconsin, the prehistoric Michigan plots were all that were ever discovered anywhere.

Because they were remindful of English formal gardens, the unusual digs were named "garden beds." But experts agreed early on that, because of their detail, accuracy and symmetry, these ancient garden beds were not used for ordinary agriculture. They had a very special purpose and meaning to whoever constructed them. The creators also had artistic and conceptual skills well beyond those of any known prehistoric Michigan culture. By comparison the Hopewell Indians, thought by most experts to be the most advanced prehistoric Michiganians, constructed only relatively crude dome-shaped burial mounds.

The unknown residents or visitors who created the garden beds abandoned them without leaving a clue as to who they were and when and why they built them. By counting growth rings on trees that had taken root on some of the plots, one early researcher estimated the beds were last used around the time Columbus first set sail for the New World. But subsequent archaeological excavations didn't turn up a single bone, piece of pottery, arrowhead, or any relic or further evidence of any kind. As a result no one has ever been able to link Michigan's mysterious garden beds to any known Native American culture.

And probably they never will. Every one of the ancient plots has been plowed under or otherwise obliterated.

FINAL VOYAGE

In August 1679 the *Griffin* became the first ship to sail the waters of the upper Great Lakes. A month later the *Griffin* became the first ship to vanish from the waters of the upper Great Lakes.

The mystery of the missing ship has become a staple of Great Lakes lore, and speculation over the fate of the wooden sailing vessel and its crew has spawned stories of mutiny and massacre. Indian legends tell of a ghostly *Griffin* seen on stormy nights, with all sails set, fighting through the waves of Lake Michigan. The *Griffin*'s ghost, according to the legend, is doomed to sail forever, unable to rest on the bottom because of the violent nature of its demise.

Nevertheless, hundreds, perhaps thousands, of explorers have probed the depths and reaches of the northern Great Lakes for the ship's remains. They are not treasure hunters. The *Griffin* is not loaded with gold bullion or other valuable cargo. Most of the searchers are nautical detectives determined to solve the nagging three-centuries-old mystery — where and how was the *Griffin* lost?

The fact that the *Griffin* was built for and commanded by the famous French explorer Robert Cavelier de la Salle makes the search even more compelling. During the late 1670s, La Salle prepared for a major expedition from Montreal, Canada, westward through the Great Lakes region and on to the Mississippi River. His plans required a cargo vessel to bring needed supplies and trade goods into that unexplored area.

During the winter of 1679, in a small clearing in the wilderness above Niagara Falls, La Salle's crew laid a keel and, from hand-hewn logs cut in the New York forest, constructed a sailboat 50-60 feet long, with a capacity of about 45 tuns (barrels).

On August 7, 1679, the first commercial vessel in the New World set sail on all-but-unknown, uncharted waters. Jutting from the ship's prow was a carved figure of a Griffin, the mythological Greek monster with the body of a lion and the head and wings of an eagle. Among the 34 men aboard was Father Louis Hennepin, who kept a diary of the *Griffin*'s maiden voyage.

The tiny ship headed up the Niagara River and out onto the shallow waters of Lake Erie. Three days later, according to Hennepin's account, the *Griffin* anchored at the mouth of the Detroit River, where fresh bear meat and other wild game was loaded aboard. The voyage continued up Lake St. Clair, the St. Clair River and into Lake Huron. On August 27, La Salle and his men entered the Straits of Mackinac and anchored the *Griffin* in a bay near present-day St. Ignace. After resting for a week at the small settlement — which included a Jesuit mission, two Indian villages, and a small group of French traders — they set sail west across Lake Michigan. A day later the *Griffin* again anchored, this time in a bay formed by one of many islands that line the entrance to Wisconsin's Green Bay. For the next several days, the ship was loaded with pelts obtained in trade from local Indians.

Against the advice of his captain and others, La Salle then ordered the *Griffin* and its cargo back to New York. There, the crew was to sell the furs and use the money to purchase additional supplies La Salle felt he needed before continuing his trek westward to the Mississippi. La Salle would head a party, which included Father Hennepin, that would remain and explore the Wisconsin wilderness. In the spring they would meet the *Griffin* at present-day St. Joseph, Michigan.

On September 18 the *Griffin*, carrying pilot Luc the Dane and five sailors, fired a ceremonial cannon shot and, powered by favorable, light westerly winds, set sail for Niagara.

La Salle and his expedition paddled canoes south down the Wisconsin shore, around the southern end of Lake Michigan, and arrived at St. Joseph on November 1. The *Griffin*, however, didn't show up as planned.

The following spring the *Griffin* didn't show up as planned. La-Sallle sent two men to search for signs of his supply ship while he remained at St. Joseph and constructed a fort. After making a complete circuit of Lake Michigan, the men reported that they "had neither seen . . . nor heard tidings of (the *Griffin*)."

Father Hennepin remained in the Great Lakes region for several years after the *Griffin*'s disappearance and he, too, heard no information or even rumors about the fate of the vessel. Evidently, no wreckage or bodies had washed up anywhere along shoreline that was, for the times, regularly passed by Indians and French fur traders in canoes.

The *Griffin* and its crew had vanished? But how?

One theory has it that during a storm the ship took shelter in a bay, where it was boarded by Indians who killed the crew and burned the ship.

A variation says that the crew turned traitor, landed, sold the cargo, scuttled the ship, and went inland, only to be killed by Indians.

Most investigators then and now, however, believe that the *Griffin* and its crew perished and sank in a terrible several-day-long storm that began the night they left Green Bay. What's left of the *Griffin*, they say, may still rest somewhere on the northern Great Lakes bottom.

That possibility has sent countless divers to areas, carefully calculated or simply guessed, where the *Griffin* may have gone down.

After more than three centuries, the desire to find La Salle's ship is still so intense it seems as though every splinter of wood wreckage found anywhere on the northern Great Lakes is first speculated to have come from the *Griffin*. As recently as the 1980s, near just one island — Manitoulin, in Georgian Bay — three different wrecks all were initially labeled as possibly being the *Griffin*.

Trouble is, the *Griffin* was only the first of hundreds of wooden ships to perish on the northern Great Lakes. And even when viewed with sophisticated instruments and devices, the wreckage of one still looks pretty much like that of any other. If we have found or ever do find the *Griffin*, we probably won't know for sure.

WHY "WOLVERINES"?

A long-standing unexplained Michigan mystery is how or why our state came to be known as the "Wolverine State" and its residents nicknamed "wolverines."

Not many Michiganians know what a wolverine is or what it looks like. Weighing about 25-30 pounds, wolverines are the largest members of the weasel family, which includes weasels, of course, plus martens, fishers and badgers. The wolverine's most attractive feature is its deep-brown fur marked with bands of chestnut along the sides plus irregular yellowish-white spots or patches. Otherwise, as former *Detroit Free Press* outdoor writer Tom Opre once quoted from an old hunting magazine, the animal looks like it is ". . . made up of a rather misfit collection of cast-off or leftover parts from other animals. Take the ears of a raccoon, the head of a small dog, . . . the feet of a bear, (and) the legs of a badger. . . ." The wolverine is not cute and cuddly.

Nor has the powerful, intelligent animal been blessed with a pleasing personality. Like a skunk it can expel a foul-looking yellowish musk with an odor to match. Wolverines come out at night to feed on plants or animal flesh — alive, dead or decayed, no matter — and will gorge until stuffed. Then the animal eats some more. In short, the wolverine has earned a reputation as a vicious, ugly glutton.

The reason most Michiganians aren't familiar with the animal is that there are probably none in the wild in Michigan now, and experts disagree on whether there *ever* have been any in the state. A few may have filtered into the Upper Peninsula from their favored Canadian habitat, but not many. A DNR expert says that, since each male wolverine carves out a territory that can be 80 to 100 miles from end to end, the entire U.P. could support no more than 12 mated pairs.

So while not many, if any, wolverines ever roamed Michigan, at one time we were a clearinghouse for piles of wolverine *pelts*. And that has given rise to a couple of plausible explanations for our nickname. During the fur-trading era, roughly from 1700-1800, trappers from Ontario, Minnesota and Wisconsin brought animal skins to major trading posts at Sault Ste. Marie and the Mackinac area. From there the pelts — including, according to old records, those of wolverines — were shipped to Detroit, on to Atlantic Coast ports, and from there to Europe.

Some say that because of the great number of wolverine furs coming from northern Michigan, shippers along the Atlantic Coast began to refer to the area as the "Wolverine Territory." Another theory has it that not only was it the abundance of the furs, but also the body odors of the chronically unbathed post owners that caused fur brokers to begin referring to the posts' proprietors as "wolverines."

Even less-complimentary speculations involve the animal's repulsive character. In 1835 residents of both Michigan and Ohio prepared to battle for possession of a strip of land that included the city of Toledo. Though now known as the Toledo "War," the border dispute turned out to be, in the spectrum of history, little more than a loud argument and some name-calling. The Ohioans labeled their adversaries "wolverines:—possibly for the first time—because Michigan residents, they claimed, were so "bloodthirsty, vicious, smelly and ugly."

Some historians believe we were disparaged even earlier. They say that when the first American settlers moved into Michigan and pushed Indians off their land, the Native Americans called the newcomers "wolverines," because the land-grabbers reminded them of the gluttonous animal they hated.

Yet another piece of folklore involves Conrad Ten Eyck, who in the early 1800s built a tavern and inn on a sandy knoll above the River Rouge near present-day Dearborn. Each night Ten Eyck's establishment was filled with homesteaders on their way to other parts of Michigan. The boisterous innkeeper, known as "Old Coon," liked to tease his guests, or perhaps tried to impress them with the wilds of Michigan by shouting to his wife, "Sally, put on some more wolf steaks." As the story goes, upon leaving the dining room one evening, a pretty young woman asked coyly, "Did I really have wolf steak?" When Ten Eyck said she most assuredly had, she retorted, "Well, then I guess that makes me a wolverine." Ten Eyck liked the comeback so much that, from then on, he told all settlers who passed through his inn that they were "wolverines."

In a way, it doesn't matter when, how or why we were first called "wolverines," because the nickname isn't official anyway. Not only that, the wolverine isn't even Michigan's official state animal. We don't have one.

WAS A MICHIGAN MAN THE FIRST TO FLY?

Several questions make up the historical mystery that surrounds Michigan's first aviator, Augustus Moore Herring. Was he the first person in the *world* to fly a powered airplane? Did he beat the Wright Brothers into the air by more than five years? And if so why hasn't he been credited with the distinction?

There's no doubt that Herring was an influential aviation pioneer, and as such most of his life has been fairly well chronicled. Born August 3, 1867, in Georgia, from early boyhood he was "obsessed with the idea that man ought to fly," according to a 1908 article in *Harper's Weekly*. The son of a wealthy cotton merchant, Herring could afford to indulge that interest by studying engineering, first in Europe and then at the Stevens Institute in New York. In 1888 he wrote a thesis at Stevens titled, "The Flying Machine as a Mechanical Engineering Problem." When the university refused to accept a paper dealing with such a preposterous concept, Herring dropped out of school and never returned or graduated.

Instead, he began practical, hands-on work and wrote hundreds of articles for both scientific journals and the lay press. His writings caught the attention of scientists at the Smithsonian Institution in Washington, D.C., and for a few months in 1895 Herring was placed in charge of "flying machine experiments" at the prestigious facility. In 1896 he abruptly left for Chicago, where he assisted the respected French civil engineer Octave Chanute in glider experiments. Over the next several months, the pair made several successful glider flights out over the Lake Michigan sand dunes near Gary, Indiana.

But Herring did not want to depend on the breezes to be able to fly. He began developing compressed-air engines he believed eventually could power and lift flying machines. Convinced his concept was sound, Herring applied for a U.S. patent on an "aeroplane" in 1896. Again he suffered rejection, this time because, said the patent examiner, "the entire invention rests on a theory that has never been proven."

Herring, however, pressed on. Not wishing to work further with or compete with Chanute, he moved to St. Joseph, Michigan, in 1897. There, he set up a motorcycle-shop business and continued his flying experiments. At the same time, he obtained critical financial backing from Matthias Arnot, a banker from New York.

Over the next several months, Herring constructed a self-designed biplane-type glider. He assembled a bamboo pole frame then covered it with a muslin skin. Each of the craft's two 56-inch-wide wings arched 18 feet from tip to tip. Mounted flush with the lower wing was a 12-lb., two-cylinder compressed-air motor that powered twin 5-foot-diameter propellers. In October 1898 Herring was finally ready to test his machine . . . and his lifelong dream.

Trouble was, not many people cared, and that may have cost both Herring and Michigan a prominent, even singular place in aviation history. At the time all inventors, but especially those who thought they could fly, were considered eccentric or flat-out crazy. The residents of St. Joseph and just about everyone else largely ignored Augustus Moore Herring and his work.

On October 11, 1898, at Silver Beach, Herring probably attempted his first powered flight. His only witness, however, was his financial backer, Arnot. The two men claimed that Herring managed to get his motorized glider to skim over some 50 feet of Lake Michigan sand beaches. But they couldn't prove it.

So Herring invited Octave Chanute and Dr. A. F. Zahn, an aviation expert from the Naval Laboratory in Washington, D.C., to witness a second flight. When the two men showed up, on October 16, Herring couldn't get his compressed-air engine to work properly and was unable to get his plane off the ground. The next day the glider was damaged, and both of the would-be reliable witnesses left town even more skeptical of Herring's claims.

Herring did not give up. He repaired his plane, and on October 22 he gathered together two newspaper reporters and a few friends to witness another attempt. Herring and his small entourage walked down Broad Street to the beach. Several young boys followed far behind and then hid behind some bushes to see what the "professor," as they called Herring, was going to do. "Everyone thought he was a little cuckoo," recalled one of the youngsters 60 years later. "But we got a kick out of watching him."

Herring opened the door to the Silver Beach amusement park's dance pavilion, and disappeared inside. More than a month before, the building had been closed for the winter, and Herring had used it as a convenient place to work on and store his plane.

In a few moments he emerged carrying the light glider on his back. After using a gasoline-fueled compressor to fill the air tank on his plane's motor, he crawled under the craft and lifted it easily onto his shoulders. He then opened a valve, the motor roared, and the propellers spun. Herring took two or three steps and according to all witnesses, including the awestruck boys, went airborne clinging to a bar at the bottom of the plane.

"(Herring) succeeded in making a flight of upwards of 70 feet against a strong northerly wind. . . . During the flight, which lasted some eight to ten seconds, Prof. Herring's feet seemed to almost graze the ground while the machine skimmed along on a level path over the beach. The landing was characterized by a slight turning to the left and slowing of the engine, when the machine and operator came as gently to rest on the sand as a bird instinct with life." So wrote a reporter in the October 24, 1898, edition of the *Benton Harbor Evening News*.

The first-person description of the flight also observed that, "It is probably the first time in the world's history that a true flying machine . . . has ever carried its operator in successful flight."

Herring might have become a history book headliner except for an incredible oversight on the part of everyone present. No one, not even the reporters, took a photograph of Herring in flight. Matthias Arnot, Herring's financial backer, almost did. He stood motionless, too stunned he later said, to snap a picture until the very end. Thus, the only photo of the Herring flight shows him sitting under his plane just as he landed.

In the absence of convincing evidence to back up Herring's claim to the world's first airplane flight, Orville and Wilbur Wright were credited with the feat more than five years later, in December 1903. Ironically, Herring visited the Wrights in 1900 and built them a glider, which they flew. Some historians say it may have been the first time the Wright brothers ever went into the air.

Herring himself persisted in his attempts to succeed at powered flight and still might have beaten the Wright brothers. But a terrible fire in 1901 literally sent everything in his project, from plans to planes, up in smoke. He suffered more business and personal setbacks until his death, in 1926 in New York.

We'll probably never know for certain whether Herring really did leave the ground that October day in 1898. In the last 20 years, though, some aviation historians have grudgingly admitted that it's possible, maybe even likely.

But they are still unwilling to credit Herring with a significant first. A 1977 Royal Aeronautics Society of London publication, for instance, said that even if ". . . Herring did become airborne in a powered machine, if ever so briefly, before the Wrights' four flights . . . (he did not) achieve sustained and controlled flight. It is the words 'sustained' and 'controlled' that mark the difference."

Thomas J. Millar, a St. Joseph area pilot and aviation history enthusiast, believes Herring deserves fame not footnote and says it all boils down to semantics. "I don't care how short it was or how long it was or how high it was, you are either flying or you're not," he says.

HOW MUCH GOLD IN THEM THAR MICHIGAN HILLS?

There's no question that there *is* gold in Michigan. Gold discoveries have been documented in as many as 100 places scattered throughout 27 Lower Peninsula counties. And in the Upper Peninsula near Ishpeming, there is a small gold "range" that was worked by as many as 11 different mines in the late 1800s. During that Michigan "gold rush," a special railroad track was built to a station named Golden, and a nugget from one mine was exhibited at the 1893 Chicago World's Fair.

But all of the U.P. mines closed before 1900, and the Lower Peninsula finds have never amounted to much. Yet thousands of treasure hunters and others still wonder, is there — if not a fantastic "mother lode" of gold — at least enough of the precious metal hidden out there somewhere in Michigan to make some lucky prospector or company rich?

Most experts say no. True, the western U.P. probably has undiscovered veins of gold embedded in its 2.7-billion-year-old volcanic rock. But because of the rugged terrain and the erratic nature of those deposits, probably no one will ever find a lode large enough to profitably mine. And in the Lower Peninsula, say geologists, where gold is found it is so thinly scattered through sand and gravel that the largest "nugget" you could expect to find would be a flake not much bigger than the head of a pin.

On the other hand, Dearborn's MARC Geologic Research Service says in its 1986 publication, *Gold in Michigan*, "(No commercial-size deposits) of gold have been found in the Lower Peninsula. This does not mean that there are none present; just that none have been found."

Lower Peninsula gold is "placer gold," that is scrapings of U.P. gold carried by glaciers and dumped below the Straits some 12,000 years ago. Most Lower Peninsula gold that has been found has been panned from streams. Since placer gold can vary in size from flakes to nuggets, there is the remote possibility that a marble-size or larger chunk may be lying on a stream bottom. Or even better, perhaps the glaciers picked up and dropped a gold-filled boulder, from which particles continue to flake off and move downstream. Some lucky or persistent panner might be able to trace the placer gold deposits upstream to that big-bucks source.

It's those germs of hope that develop into full-blown gold fever for some modern-day prospectors who — using century-old state geologist reports and ultra high-tech metal detectors — pull on waders and set out to strike it rich. For most it's a hobby. For a few it consumes instead of makes fortunes.

Some seekers are further spurred by apocryphal stories about fabulous finds. Around 1900, for instance, an old man supposedly made a fortune panning gold from dirt dug near Harrisville. However, nobody knows where, or who he was, or what happened to him. Gold fields near Alpena in the 1920s and at Vernon, Perry, Ortonville, Montrose, Grand Rapids and other areas during the Depression all turned out to be scams. Recently, a story circulated about a University of Michigan professor who figured out a way to sluice enough gold from the Huron River to pay his children's college bills.

And that's the secret to getting rich from Lower Peninsula gold, say some dedicated fortune seekers. It's just a matter of developing the right process to profitably extract the one part gold from three million parts sand. In the mid-1960s four men, including a state highway department expert on sand and gravel, invested hundreds of thousands of dollars and 10 years of their lives in an attempt to do just that. They did find gold in 90 Lower Peninsula gravel pits, and one year they even managed to extract $101 worth. But it cost them $20,000 to do it, and the company folded not long after.

Still, because there's no doubt that gold exists in Michigan, there's also no doubt that others will follow in their footsteps. Gold's glitter will continue to lure those who hope to someday, somewhere in Michigan scream, "Eureka!"

ARTFUL BUDGET CUTTING

When workers began a $45 million restoration of our state's domed capitol, all they had planned to uncover were the fine, rich details that had been hidden by a 140 years' worth of paint, wallpaper and other remodeling. But they also revealed a minor, but intriguing and confusing historical mystery.

In 1989 when William Seale, a consultant who specializes in Victorian-era furnishings, examined the Capitol's collection of 35 paintings, some more than a century and a half old, one in particular caught his eye — a portrait of Lewis Cass.

Cass spent a lengthy and distinguished political career in the early to mid-1800s, serving variously as Michigan territorial governor, United States senator, secretary of state, secretary of war, ambassador to France, and the Democrat's candidate for president in 1848. Most historians give Cass major credit for preparing Michigan for statehood, and some have even called him the "father of Michigan." So it wasn't unusual that his 6- by 9-foot portrait was included in the state's small collection.

What caught Seale's trained, keen eye, however, was the background in Cass' "elder-statesman" pose. It was the East Room of the White House, set as it was during George Washington's era. Cass did serve at the White House, as secretary of war and, 25 years later, state. So he may very well have had occasion to stand in the East Room, but it would have been some 50 years after George Washington was president. Seale at first theorized that whoever had done the painting had simply copied the background from the most famous likeness of Washington—the Lansdowne Portrait by Gilbert Stuart, painted in the 1790s.

Restorers at the Detroit Institute of Art (DIA) shed more light on the painting, which cast shadows on its origin. In July 1989 the dirty and torn Cass canvas was sent to the DIA to be cleaned and repaired. When, in the process, laboratory technicians routinely examined it with X-rays, a ghostly silhouette resembling George Washington's head, including his familiar wig, appeared on the negative. Alfred Acerman, the lab's painting conservator, examined the painting closely and discovered a definite change in design around Cass' head, evidenced by a build-up of lead-white paint. He also said he detected possible changes in the location of the eyes and nose.

Had someone painted over the face of the father of our country with the likeness of the father of our state? If so, who and why?

Not everyone was convinced that the shadowy image revealed by the X-rays was, in fact, Washington's. Maria Quinlan Leiby — curator of the collections at the Michigan Historical Museum, which looks after the Capitol's portraits — said she was "very skeptical" of the theory that someone had painted Cass' face over Washington's. First, she said the portrait really doesn't look much like Cass. The extra layers of paint, the overpainting, she speculated, may have resulted from the frustrated artist's attempts to make Cass' face look more lifelike. Plus, she added, "George Washington was such an honored figure that I find it hard to believe officials of the time would have permitted it."

But Leiby, an historian, did admit that, "It's not without precedent that paintings have been overpainted."

The investigation was further complicated by the fact that the Capitol's inventory included two paintings of Cass — the "elder statesman" pose and another depicting him as a young man. Both works are unsigned. According to records an artist named Robert McCleland painted one in the early 1830s, most likely the younger Cass, experts believe.

No one had any idea, however, who had painted the mystery "elder statesman" canvas. But they did have an idea of when. Officials discovered that in the mid-1940s a portrait of George Washington in the Capitol's inventory had vanished without a trace.

Why might some artist have secretly taken the Washington canvas and painted in Cass' face. It certainly wasn't an elaborate for-profit art hoax. "Sounds like a cost-saving measure to me," said Sen. William Sederberg, R-East Lansing, chairman of the committee handling the Capitol restoration. Historian Seale, whose observation had opened the mini-mystery, said, "It would be so typical of a state — a little thrift there."

In the end the controversial Cass portrait was cleaned and returned to the Senate chambers in 1990.

If Cass' face does hide Washington's, George got poetic or political justice in another art form. Outside of the Lewis Cass Office Building in the Lansing capitol complex is a sculpture of . . . George Washington.

WHAT'S IN A NAME?

It's not so much a mystery as it is a nagging, unsettled and, to some, unsettling question. What should we residents of Michigan properly call ourselves — Michiganians or Michiganders? After a century and a half of friendly and not so friendly debate and even political intervention, there still is no definite or official preference.

The few Michigan residents of the early 1800s didn't have a choice and probably didn't care. If you lived in the Michigan Territory, you were referred to by outsiders as a "Michiganian." The term probably first appeared in print in 1813, according to one Michigan historian. And during the 1830s, as Michigan worked toward and then obtained statehood, "Michiganian" showed up in the written accounts of literary Easterners who had visited here.

But in 1848 Abraham Lincoln, of all people, complicated the issue. The Democrats' nominee for president that election year was Lewis Cass, Michigan's first nationally prominent politician. Lincoln was a member of the opposition Whigs. In an early version of a negative campaign ad, Lincoln sarcastically referred to Cass as that "great Michi-gander." "Gander," according to the dictionary and common usage of the time, meant a "simpleton or halfwit." Lincoln's well-publicized remark helped cost Cass the election and the

179

presidency.

The derogatory moniker evidently didn't bother some Michigan residents, however, because they began calling themselves "Michigander," thus launching an ongoing conflict with Michiganians.

Today, "Michiganian" still seems to be the choice of those in the know. Eminent Michigan historian George May, for instance, says that " 'Michiganian' is more sensible and consistent with the form employed in referring to residents of most other states." And long-time Michigan Secretary of State Richard Austin has stated that " 'Michiganian' is now the accepted term."

Michiganians are also quick to point out, as Lincoln did, the link between "gander" and subpar intelligence. Even the main dictionary definition, a male goose, they say, is crude, unflattering and sexist. A Detroit newspaper editorial once suggested that we might put bumper stickers on our cars urging Michiganders to "honk if they love Michigan."

"Michigander," however, seems to be the people's choice. In 1983, for instance, *Michigan Natural Resources* magazine conducted a poll of its readers. "Michigander" was the choice over "Michiganian" 5 to 1. Two years later the *Detroit Free Press* not only conducted a call-in poll, but also agreed to abide by the results. Out of nearly 3,000 votes cast, "Michigander" won out by a mere 71 votes. But true to its word, the *Free Press* began referring and still refers to Michigan residents as "Michiganders" in its articles.

And Michiganders aren't shy about taking pot shots of their own at the term "Michiganian." "It sounds like someone with acne," says Hall of Fame broadcaster J.P. McCarthy of WJR radio, Detroit. A respondent to the *Free Press* poll was even harsher saying, "Michiganian sounds like a venereal disease." "It's a wimpy term," said another caller. "You have to whine when you say it."

The state legislature attempted to end the bickering but only succeeded in raising it to a more public forum. In 1979 by a vote of 50-32, and again in 1981, 59-30, the State House of Representatives passed a resolution and a bill designating "Michiganian" as the official "patrial term" for residents of Michigan. Both times, after much debate, the measures failed to make it onto the floor of the Senate.

The pols and polls may have complicated rather than helped settle the identity crisis. Respondents and lawmakers who didn't particularly like either "Michiganian" or "Michigander" came up with their own alternatives such as "Michiganite" and "Michiganer."

Two of the most-creative suggestions, however, were only attempts to put the conflict into proper perspective. "Anyone who keeps arguing over the issue should be called a 'Michiganiac,' " suggested one man, "because they must be crazy." And an Oak Park state representative suggested "Michigos," which he said is a Jewish word meaning, "Who needs it?"

PLACE NAME INDEX

ABOUT THE AUTHOR

Gary W. Barfknecht, 48, was born and raised in Virginia, Minnesota, the "Queen City" of that state's Mesabi Iron Range. After receiving a bachelor of science degree from the University of Minnesota in 1967 and a master of science degree from the University of Washington (Seattle) in 1969, Barfknecht came to Flint, Michigan, as a paint chemist with the E.I. DuPont & deNemours company.

But after only a year on the job, Barfknecht and the chemical giant reached the mutual conclusion that he was not suited for corporate life, and Barfknecht set out on a freelance writing career. Over the next several years, his articles were featured in several national publications. He also was the ghost writer for *A Father, A Son, and a Three-Mile Run* (Zondervan, 1974) and authored a local guide book, *33 Hikes from Flint* (Friede Publications, 1975).

While freelancing, Barfknecht also managed a hockey pro shop at a Flint ice arena. That job led to a position as hockey commissioner, and in 1977, when Barfknecht took over the directorship of almost all amateur hockey programs in Genesee County, he postponed his writing efforts.

He resumed his writing career in 1981 with the release of *Michillaneous*, a collection of Michigan trivia. In 1983 Barfknecht followed with *Murder, Michigan*, which describes "the dark side of Michigan history." In 1984 he compiled *Mich-Again's Day*, a collection of Michigan history/trivia arranged in an on-this-day-in-Michigan-history format. *Michillaneous II* appeared in the state's bookstores in 1985. And Barfknecht described Michigan's most unique places to go and things to do in *Ultimate Michigan Adventures*, released May 1989.

As owner and managing editor of Friede Publications, Barfknecht has brought several other Michigan authors' books into print (see p. *iii*).

Barfknecht currently resides in Davison, Michigan, with his wife, Ann. They have two daughters — Amy, 27, and Heidi, 22.